Cases and Exercises in
Business, Finance and The Law

Dr. James J. Ravelle
Moravian College

ISBN-10: 0692760334
ISBN-13: 978-062760338

DEDICATION

To my son James

Whose courage to change his life inspired me

CONTENTS

PREFACE

It is a truth. As educators we need to provide students with an ethical and theoretical foundation in economics and business. However, majors and degrees in management, business and finance are also applied disciplines. This fundamental fact makes the educational delivery of business-related courses similar to other disciplines – such as engineering, accounting, medicine and dentistry. After all, when a student's education is complete she or he should have an idea on how to build a bridge or perform a root canal.

The purpose of this book is to provide students with a glimpse into that applied world. To that end I have chosen cases and exercises, which are rooted and derived from real world situations. The micro-society of the organization is a true reflection of the complications and complexity of that world in which students reside and will take their part. Sometimes it represents the humor and craziness of that world as well. Most of the cases are inspired by true events. Often they are individually specific or an amalgam of business problems that have happened. Most are rooted from matters in the author's experience. A few are based upon business events exposed in the public arena. In most cases, the names of people and places have been purposely changed (except at times for the author) to avoid the disclosure of information that they would wish to remain private.

This book is meant as a supplement to those courses in business, finance and the law for which it may be relevant. It does not replace a textbook but rather gives textbooks context and meaning. It is hoped that the use of these cases will challenge students to think and help them act rationally and ethically as they study and face the organizational world in which we really live. It is the author's hope that the book will also have the spillover benefit of increasing a student's motivation to learn.

No book can really be written alone. Any author needs help and inspiration. Most of all, I wish to thank Laura Hunter, my summer assistant and co-editor for her invaluable assistance. It was quite a summer project and her help went beyond the call of duty. I especially want to thank Dr. Gary Kaskowitz, Dean of the Division of Arts, Humanities and Social Sciences at Moravian College. His help was valuable in too many ways to list. I wish to acknowledge the support of my family – thank you Emily, JJ and Gabriel. And a "special" thanks goes to my favorite colleague and love of my life, Dr. Linda L. Ravelle.

James J. Ravelle
Bethlehem, Pennsylvania
August 2016

CHAPTER 1
CONTRACTS AND SALES

Case 1A
Ladies of the Ring

Stacy had lived all her life in Bethlehem, Pennsylvania. She had very few relatives in the area. Her mom and dad were originally from Indiana and had moved to the Lehigh Valley after her dad was transferred. She was an only child and had no cousins, or aunts and uncles nearby. She went to a small Liberal Arts College in town and while there became part of a social sorority and developed a close bond with the other members. They really did become like sisters. During college she met a guy from nearby Knee High University. He too was from the local area. Maybe he was a bit overweight and he might not be the most handsome man in the world, but he was funny and he flew his own plane. He and his college friends had the most outrageously fun parties, although they did tend to drink too much. Two years after college they were still dating. Stacy knew that her friends didn't care much for Tim Macy, but she felt like she had a family with him and that was what really mattered to her.

Tim called early in the afternoon one Friday. "Stacy, pick your favorite restaurant. I want this evening to be special for us," he said. Stacy agreed to meet Tim at the Aspen Inn at 7 o'clock that evening. It had been a long day and she was tired, but Tim seemed especially excited when he saw her at dinner. When dessert came, Tim ordered for them and excused himself. The waiter served rainbow sherbet with a waffle cookie. Stacy didn't mind sherbet, but she had never expressed any particular fondness for it. As she and Tim dug in, she bit onto something hard on her spoon. "Tim, look at this! It's a ring and I almost swallowed it," she exclaimed. Tim suggested that she wash it off with some water and she did so. The ring was beautiful. It was clearly solid gold and had a blister of large and colorful diamonds in the middle. "My

2

god, it's beautiful!" exclaimed Stacy. She could tell that it was an engagement ring and that Tim had planned the entire thing. Tim asked her, "What do you think, should we do this?" Stacy simply said, "Yes I will." "Good," said Tim, "Because I want you to have that ring." Tim and Stacy were engaged.

Wedding plans were not the only thing on Stacy's mind. Tim came from a very well to do family. After college he had moved back in with his parents. Stacy was rarely there, but the time came to formally meet the family. Stacy was very impressed by the size of the family mansion in Salisbury Township. It was a little dated, but large in size and clearly had the best of everything. Tim's father was a quiet and unfriendly man and he seldom spoke to Stacy. Tim's mother was very outgoing and never seemed to stop talking. Stacy knew all about the string of cement mills owned by the family, but Tim's mother never seemed to tire of talking about how wealthy the family was and their ancestry. When she was with Tim's mother, Stacy always felt like just a common transplanted girl from Indiana. The reality was that Stacy did not really like Tim's mother and the impressive but cold house. But then again, none of her friends liked Tim either. Both sides would have to make adjustments.

As the wedding approached, Stacy was beginning to think of things beyond the honeymoon. Tim surely could not move in with her and her two-sorority sisters from college. The time had come to discuss the matter of where they were going to live and if they would rent or buy a home after the wedding. Stacy showed Tim some literature for new townhouses being built in the area. She asked if Tim would consider new construction. Tim quickly replied "Stacy, are you crazy? You are going to move in with me at my family's house after the wedding." Stacy was annoyed at this suggestion. "For how long, Tim?" she asked. Tim said, "well forever". Mother would never let us live anywhere else. By the way, mother told me to tell you that she will plan the entire wedding, down to your gown and bridesmaids. She doesn't like the direction you have been taking things." This troubled Stacy. After a few days of thinking about everything, she called Tim and told him that the wedding was off. She wasn't even sure she wanted to see him again.

Two weeks after the split Stacy came home from an exercise class and received a call from Mrs. Macy. She said, "Young woman, I need to have a talk with you. You will meet me in exactly one hour at the Hotel Bethlehem for lunch." Stacy felt a sense of dread, but decided to face the music. When they met, it was even worse than she had expected. Tim's mother spent most of the time tearing her apart and making her feel bad. Stacy was on the verge of tears throughout the one-sided conversation. "And one more thing you little tramp!" she demanded. "You will return the ring my son gave you. It was a family heirloom, handcrafted in 1878 by Tiffany's in New York. It is priceless to us. You will return it to me with a note of apology for the pain you caused our family or I will have you arrested." With that final insult, Tim's mother threw thirty dollars on the table to pay for lunch and left the hotel.

Stacy was afraid. Would she really be arrested if she didn't return the ring? She had planned to return it all along, but now she was getting mad. It wasn't right to treat anyone that way. Stacy picked up the phone and called the one person in the world whom she trusted the most, James Parnell, an attorney and faculty advisor to her college sorority. Parnell told her not to return the ring or do anything for that matter, until they spoke.

Challenge Questions:

1. When Tim gave Stacy the ring, was it a conditional gift or an absolute one?

2. If you were Stacy, would you return the ring even if your attorney advised you that you were not compelled to do so by the law? (The Moral Issue).

Case 1B
One Cool Investigator

Basil Duke was a civil investigator for Philadelphia Legal Services. It seemed to James Parnell and his office mate, Tammy Bender, that Basil knew everyone in and everything about Philadelphia. Tammy and Parnell were litigating a difficult and highly publicized lawsuit file against the city controller on behalf of a part-time city sanitation employee. The employee, Ray Jennick, had led a march in support of Democratic Mayor, Hank Fizzo. The controller was part of a faction of the Democratic Party in the city that opposed the mayor. They hoped to replace him in the next election with one of their own (Fizzo would later return as a republican). The controller saw Ray on the 5 o'clock news leading the demonstration and read in the Philadelphia Chronicle that Ray was a city employee. The controller sent a letter to Ray, firing him for violating the city's "Hatch Act," which forbids participation in politics by public employees. It was clear to Tammy and Parnell that Carol Mussorski, a reporter for the Chronicle, had confidential sources within the city government and that she had much more information about the case than PLS had. If Parnell could get Carol to testify as to her sources, he could prove in court that the controller's actions were politically motivated and that Ray's termination was wrongful. Ray was supporting a wife and four children and he said that he really needed to recover the monetary damages from this wrongful termination case. Parnell and Tammy were hoping to win the case and get him the money he deserved.

Parnell was given the task of serving a subpoena to Carol. Innocently, he walked over to the Chronicle's building on Market Street, noticed that Carol's office was on the sixth floor and proceeded to the elevator to get there. A security guard saw him and asked what the business was. Parnell answered honestly. After completing his laugh, the guard told Parnell to "get his a** off the premises" and that service of a subpoena to the newspaper reporters was completely forbidden at the Chronicle's offices. On another attempt, Parnell tried to walk up the fire escape behind the building and was almost on the sixth floor, when he was noticed by security. After a brief chase down the escape, he managed to get away.

Parnell needed a new game plan. Parnell and Tammy discovered Carol's address. She lived in a townhouse on Spring Garden Street in the city. They decided they would wait in the shrubbery outside her place and when she came home from work, they would serve the subpoena. Parnell spent all night hiding out, but Carol did not return. Parnell saw some things that night in Philadelphia that made him glad that he was hiding. He knew he couldn't bear to have that experience again. Frustrated, Parnell and Tammy were overheard talking about their dilemma. With Carol's testimony they would win, without it they would lose. It was that simple. But how do they serve the subpoena and make her appear? Basil, hearing the conversation, came into their office. "Are you talking about Carol Mussorski?" Basil continued, "If you are, no problem, I used to date her." Tammy wondered out loud, "Basil is there any woman in Philadelphia that you haven't dated?" For some reason, women loved Basil and he dated many. "Look, if you want, I will call Carol and ask her out. She adores me, you can serve the subpoena when we see each other," he suggested. Parnell agreed.

Basil agreed to meet Carol at 7 o'clock after work that Friday at the restaurant in the Vacation Inn in the recently restored waterfront area of the city. Carol showed up nicely dressed, coifed, and happy to see Basil again. The couple ordered drinks before dinner and talked about old times. After the drinks came, Parnell stepped from the lobby of the hotel into the restaurant and said, "Are you Carol Mussorski?" Carol said yes. "Here is a subpoena to appear in court to testify in the Ray Jennick case on Thursday at 10 am." All of the sudden, it occurred to Carol that she had been set up. She picked up her drink, turned to Basil, and threw it in his face. As she walked out, Basil wiped himself off with a cloth napkin and smiled at Parnell. They had accomplished their mission.

After winning the case, Parnell and Tammy were discussing the aftermath when Basil came into the office again. Basil asked, "How well do you know Ray Jennick?" Parnell replied that this was the first case they had with him and that he had completed the affidavit of eligibility for free legal services from PLS. According to his affidavit, his part-time earnings from the city and his net worth were below the limits required to consider him poor. "Poor my donkey!" Basil exclaimed. "Did you ever hear of Jennick Construction, Inc.?" Neither Parnell nor Tammy had. Basil continued, "Jennick Construction is one of the biggest private contractors in the city and Ray inherited the business from his grandfather over a year ago when the old man died. He is worth millions now and is just ripping us off for free legal services. What a con man he is!"

Parnell and Tammy were stunned. They had given their all to win this highly publicized case and had made enemies in the mix. It just wasn't right for Jennick to get away with this and be unjustly benefited from their services.

Challenge Questions:

1. Why isn't the relationship between Ray Jennick and Philadelphia Legal Services a contractual one?

2. How does the concept of "Quasi-Contract" apply to this fact situation?

3. In your opinion, was it inappropriate for Parnell to use Basil to help serve the subpoena in this manner? (The Moral Issue).

Case 1C
Ajax Comes Home

He was in all sense of the word, a mutt. His parents had no pedigrees but Ajax the dog was a most pleasant animal. He was always playful and glad to be with his owners, James and Glenda Parnell. Both the Parnells worked and left their house in South Whitehall Township early in the morning each day. One bright beautiful morning, the front door was left open in their haste to make it to work. Who left it open was a matter of future dispute, but one thing was certain, Ajax, alone in the house and seeing a perfect October day outside, left to explore the world and enjoy its many splendors.

When the Parnells returned home that evening and realized what they had done, they frantically attempted to locate Ajax. They were unsuccessful. The Parnells, wishing for the return of their friendly dog, placed an advertisement in the local newspaper, *The Morning Crier*. They offered the sum of $200 to anyone who would help find their dog. Three days after the advertisement no one had responded and the Parnells began to lose hope.

Gabrielle (Gabby) Cramer was a college student at Crest Hill College in Allentown. The school was located about three miles southeast of the Parnells' home. One afternoon, Gabrielle was sitting at her desk trying to write a paper. She liked the view from her dorm room because it overlooked a large park-like area on the campus. A dog lover, Gabrielle had noticed a likable dog playing by himself in the fields outside her dorm, but she didn't notice an owner. The dog seemed to be by himself as he cheerfully chased birds and played in the autumn leaves. Gabby could no longer resist the temptation of taking a break from her schoolwork.

She went outside and began to engage the dog in play. The unknown dog responded with enthusiasm to this human contact. The two played together in the campus fields for well over an hour before Gabby decided to check out the dog's nametag.

The dog's tag read, "My name is Ajax and I belong to James and Glenda Parnell." It didn't take long for Gabby to realize that the dog was lost. She looked online and noticed that there was only one James Parnell in the area, and that he resided a few short miles from campus. At around dinnertime, Gabby called the number that she had obtained from her computer. A man answered and she replied, "Hello. Is this Mr. Parnell?" Parnell answered in the positive. "My name is Gabrielle Cramer. Did you lose your dog?" she asked. Parnell knew his prayers had been answered, the dog was found. Gabby explained that she was a student at Crest Hill College, where she had found the dog. Parnell offered to drive over immediately. "Don't bother Mr. Parnell, I know where you live. I once sat for a couple's children who live near you. I have a car and I need to run some errands anyway. I will be at your house within the hour," she said. True to her word, Gabrielle showed up at the Parnells' household. Ajax sprang from the backseat of Gabby's car and master and dog were tearfully reunited.

Parnell profusely thanked Gabrielle and reached into his wallet. He removed all of the money he had in it at the time, forty dollars, and offered it to Gabrielle as a gesture of his appreciation for her kind act. "No, it's ok Mr. Parnell. I don't want your money. I am just happy that I was able to help return your dog to you," she said. Gabrielle drove away with the same seven dollars she had in her purse prior to her visit.

Challenge Questions:

1. Assume that Gabrielle returned to Crest Hill College and told her roommate about the events of the day. If her roommate had read *The Morning Crier*, had seen the reward offer and told Gabby about it, could Gabby claim the reward money under the Law of Contracts? In other words, is Gabrielle entitled to the reward money?

2. Explain what is meant by a "Unilateral Contract" and how might this concept apply to this case?

3. If you were Parnell, would you have paid Gabrielle the $200 reward simply because it was the right thing to do? (The Moral Issue).

Case Exercise 1D
The Common Law vs. the Uniform Commercial Code

The student who has the largest number of correct answers wins!

1.   After another one of her many wild parties, Carley decides to replace her floor carpets. She travels to George's Discount Carpets and purchases brand new burgundy rugs. The sale between Carley and George is governed by the
_____ UCC
_____ Common Law

2.   Maddy is concerned about the quality of her softball skills. She decides to hire Bat Mittl as a personal coach and trainer. The contract between Maddy and Bat is governed by
_____ UCC
_____ Common Law

3. Maddy also decides she wants a new look and style. She heads to Zach's Hair and Make-Up Emporium for a complete make over. Zach promises to use the latest in beauty techniques as well as hair dyes and rinses. Which set of laws apply to Maddy's make-over
_____ UCC
_____ Common Law

4.   Josh decides that GE looks like a good investment. He enters an online trade to purchase 2,000 shares of GE common through his brokerage account at Federico Investments. The relationship between Josh and Federico Investments is governed by
_____ UCC
_____ Common Law

5. Kyle is all stressed out from his job as a circus clown for the Northampton Valley Circus. He buys a vacation package, including airfare to the port of departure and cruise tickets, and decides to sail to the Bahamas. The law that applies to his vacation purchase is

_____ UCC

_____ Common Law

6. Brielle, Chelsea, and Lindsay form a landscaping business called the Sigma Lawn Service. Their first customer is James Parnell. Parnell agrees to pay Sigma the sum of $450.00 to rake the leaves and cut his easy-to-mow lawn. This relationship is covered by

_____ UCC

_____ Common Law

7. Jennifer goes to Wingman's Food Markets and purchases 300 donuts for Sam's birthday party. The purchase is covered by

_____ UCC

_____ Common Law

8. Kaitlyn cannot take it any more. She decides to consult with an attorney to see what she has to do to begin divorce proceedings against her unfaithful husband, Andrew. Her engagement of an attorney to represent her is covered by

_____ UCC

_____ Common Law

9. Craig buys a car from Honest Ellena's Used Car Lot. The sale of the car is governed by

_____ UCC

_____ Common Law

10. Catherine decides that she needs auto insurance or fears that she will get a citation for being uninsured. She buys a policy from the Sarah Greenbay Agency. The sale is covered by

_____ UCC

_____ Common Law

11. Baby Maria is out of control, as usual. Her parents, Anthony and Lily, decide to hire Nannies 911 to provide care to Baby Maria and to see if the Nannies will be able to reduce her traumatic fits. The deal with Nannies 911 is covered by

_____ UCC

_____ Common Law

Case Exercise 1E
The Battle of the Forms

Your fraternity "OGO Epsilon" owns a clothing store. You have ordered 500 general Greek organization t-shirts to sell to college organizations. This order was placed on a business "purchase order" form. The form was printed by the ASZ Business Form Company. On the back of the "ASZ" form, there is a provision stating that any disputes between the parties will be settled according to the Laws of Pennsylvania. You send your purchase order online to the Brady Textile Company (BTC). BTC sends back an acknowledgment using a form printed by the Zeta Printing Company. On the back of the "Zeta" form there is a clause that states that any disputes between the parties shall be settled according to the rules of the American Arbitration Association.

Challenge Question:

Explain the impact of UCC 2-207(1) and (2) on this contract for the sale of goods. How does it vary from the Common Law?

The Group with the "Best" explanation will receive points (to be determined by their instructor) toward their overall grade for the class. For this challenge, groups do not need to write a paper or prepare handouts. This is an in-class exercise.

Case 1F
Child Development

Five months after his son was born, the solicitations kept pouring in. Life insurance, financial planning for college, deals on baby food, etc. There seemed to be no limit to the amount of junk mail received by the Parnell family. One day there was a package crammed into the mailbox. A company from Long Island, New York, had a unique twist on how to improve things for the Parnells' son. The package contained a letter from a supposed expert in child development. In it, the expert explained how much smarter and psychologically advanced the Parnell child would be if his parents would expose him to the developmental books and toys contained in the package. This package also contained a plastic book with pictures of animals in it and a cloth toy that when touched, produced a squeaky sound. Parnell gave the book and the toy to his five-month-old son, who promptly proceeded to chew on both.

The company that sent the items stated that the family need not do anything to respond and that every four weeks a new "developmental" toy and book would be sent to the home and that they would be billed monthly. If the Parnells did not want the items, all they had to do was return them to the company. The next month, a new squeaky toy and plastic book was sent to the Parnells. The boy proceeded to do the same with it, namely, eat it. Parnell was amazed at how much the boy had developed with the use of the toys and books. (We are being cynical here).

That same month a bill was sent to the Parnells for the sum of $132 for the items provided to them. Parnell did not pay the bill, nor did he return the items. After a third month of receiving toys (same thing- from package to mouth), the company sent a final invoice for $198, which also was not paid.

Four months later, Parnell began to get letters from a collection agency, stating that if he did not pay the invoice, dire consequences would apply. A second collection letter was later sent, threatening the Parnells with a lawsuit.

Challenge Questions:

1. Under the law of contracts, is silence acceptance in this case?

2. How would you respond to the actions of the collection agency?

3. Since Parnell and his family had use of the books and toys, do you think it is right that they pay for them regardless of any legal obligation to do so? (The Moral Issue).

Case 1G
The Mail Box Rule

       Nina Engleman is the president of a family owned business, Engleman Commercial Construction, Inc. On behalf of the business, Nina placed an order for $500,000 of steel I beams from the Donohue Steel Company (DSC), to be used in the framing and construction of the new "Corrine Blass Athletic Complex" at Lehman College in Bayville, New Jersey. The following facts apply to this situation:

- The purchase order (PO) for the I Beams was placed in the mail on April 1st, 2015, from the company's headquarters in Honesdale, PA.
- The PO was received in the mail by DSC at West Chester, PA, on April 3rd.
- On April 4th, Lehman College went into receiverships due to financial hardship. The court's receiver immediately canceled all building contracts.
- On April 5th, DSC sent an acknowledgement accepting Nina's offer by mail from West Chester.
- On April 6th, Nina sent a revocation of the PO to DSC by mail; DSC received the revocation on April 8th.

Challenge Questions:

1. Is there a contract between Nina's company and DSC?

2. How does the "mail box" rule apply to this situation? Further, if you were Nina, how would you condition the PO?

3. If you were DSC and the enforcement of this contract might bankrupt a family business like Nina's, would you permit the cancellation of the contract? (The Moral Issue).

Case 1H
The Corker School of Etiquette

Would you use "due influence" (as opposed to undue influence) on your spouse? The following fact situation is based on a true story as revealed in a front-page story of a major newspaper.

K. Ron Corker believes that people need education, but of the most peculiar kind. Ron runs a school in the State of Texas for "gold-diggers." To gain entrance, the man or woman must be under the age of 35, attractive, and have good social skills. Eighty percent (80%) of the school's enrollment is female and twenty percent (20%) male. At the school, students take courses in etiquette, basic accounting, personal finance, estate administration, personal grooming and financial investigation. Basically, the school attempts to teach students how to identify persons who are wealthy (with a net worth in excess of $5,000,000) and who are older and perhaps, in poor health. The target person is called a 'mark.' The point of this education is to not only identify a 'mark,' but also to get the mark to fall in love with the "Corker" graduate, marry them and to leave them their entire estate at their passing, or at least obtain a generous settlement if the marriage fails. The school claims a high success rate.

Challenge Questions:

1. While this practice is legal, should it be outlawed?

2. Would you as an individual consider enrolling in the Corker School? (The Moral Issue).

Case 1I
131 Roach Street

Three college students from Knee High University decided that they had waited long enough. After living on campus for two years, they wanted to experience the freedom of living on their own. The group consisted of Ernesto, an engineering student from Kennett Square, Pa; Bart, a finance major from Gladwyn, PA; and Elmer, a marketing major from Mendham, NJ. After a brief search, the boys thought they had found what they were looking for just two blocks from Knee High's campus at 131 Roach Street. The landlord was a 38-year old real estate broker named Alexandra (called Sandy). Sandy and her partners also owned two other houses, which they rented to students. Sandy had been in the real estate business for sixteen years. The parties at first seemed to get along and the boys entered into a written lease (a lease is a type of contract for the possession of property) with Sandy for the property. The essential terms were as follows:

- The lease would begin on August 1st, 2014 and go until July 31st, 2015.
- The boys would pay $1,100 per month.
- The heating source was fuel oil- automatic deliveries of the fuel oil would be made as needed by a reputable oil service company and the boys would pay the cost of delivery as it came due.
- The boys would be responsible for all routine maintenance.
- In an event of default, the lease contained a standard acceleration clause, with a confession of judgment provision and attorney's fees provision.

The three 20 year old juniors moved in around August 15th and in their first two weeks of possession prior to the start of the semester, they had multiple parties which consisted of, for the most part, large groups of people (some of whom they did not know) drinking excessively and spilling garbage and beer on the newly installed carpet. In September, the number of parties declined, but the students lived mostly on takeout food and failed attempts to cook something. By their own admission between September 1st and October 15th, none of the boys had any recollection of ever doing the dishes. Mountains of plate-wear and plastic-wear began to pile up.

By the end of September, the students began to be troubled by a serious roach problem. Roaches seemed to be everywhere. They covered the kitchen. Their un-cleaned bedrooms and bathroom also became roach infested. The boiling point was reached when the boys noticed rather large rats (an ugly species of river rats) eating their garbage and unfinished food. Ernesto was particularly grossed out one day when he left the dinner table to answer a phone call and when he returned, found a rat eating his sausage and bacon pizza. After chasing the rat away, Ernesto was able to finish the slice.

The boys were upset and confused by the roach and rat problem, and called Sandy. She told them that she thought this was a routine maintenance problem and that they should call an exterminator and that the boys would be obliged to pay for the costs of their service. The boys were livid at this suggestion. They blamed Sandy for their pest problems. Instead of calling an exterminator, they called the Dean of Housing at Knee High to see what could be done. The Dean explained that he had no jurisdiction over off-campus housing, but that several dorm openings had become available on campus due to student departures (it was now October 15th) and that the boys were welcome to return to campus and live once again in the spatial dorm rooms, eat at the university cafeteria, and receive daily maid service. The boys called their parents and within 48 hours, took their possessions out of the rented house and into the safety and serenity of the dorms.

Sandy contacted her attorney, a tough litigation-oriented lawyer. Her attorney confessed judgment against the boys for months of unpaid rent ($11,000), damages to the property ($2,000), unpaid fuel bill ($400), attorney's fees ($3,400), and court and service costs ($200). The total judgment was for $17,000. The boys went crazy when they received the judgment notice and contacted the university, which referred them to one of the attorneys on its referral list. The attorney was also a Professor of Economics and Business at the time at a neighboring Liberal Arts College.

Challenge Questions:

1. Is the lease an example of a "contract of adhesion"?

2. What, if any, relevance does the UCC 2-302 have to this situation?

3. In your opinion, do both parties share the blame for this situation? (The Moral Issue).

Case 1J
Consideration Reconsidered

The Parnells wanted to move. Dr. Parnell, who was also an attorney as well as a Ph.D., was recently promoted to Associate Professor of Economics at a fine college at which he taught and was also granted tenure. Mrs. Parnell was an MBA student at a university in Beckham, the small town in which Dr. Parnell's college was located. The Parnells decided to sell their condo in Allenville and move to a nice house in a pleasant neighborhood in Beckham. Agreements of sale were entered and the settlement date (time for performance) of each contract was on June 30th. The Parnells knew they were cutting it close by both buying and selling on the same day, but they were young and needed to save money. At 10 am on June 30th, the closing on the Parnells' house went smoothly. Dr. Parnell handled his own settlement and the buyer was prompt and had the purchase money ready (so far so good). At 11 am, the Parnells, with the help of a few friends, loaded up their remaining possessions in their automobiles and a rental truck, and along with their 20 month-old baby, headed to Beckham for the 1 pm settlement to purchase their new home. That is when things began to unravel.

The Parnells expected to see both Sellers at the agreement. Mrs. Seller, with her attorney, was there, but Mr. Seller was nowhere to be found. After an hour or so, Dr. Parnell finally asked about the whereabouts of Mr. Seller. Mrs. Seller answered, "That jerk is in Mexico with his little girlfriend." Parnell then inquired, "How are we supposed to close without his signature on the deed and other title papers?" Mrs. Seller's attorney said, "Well I guess we can't." The Parnells had no home to which to return. They had sold their house that morning and the buyer had already taken possession.

The Parnells had several problems. First, they needed a place to live. Dr. Parnell called "Rock Randolph" the housing director at the college and he suggested that the Parnells move into the house used by the Zigma sorority. The Parnells did so, but they knew after two months they would need to move. Fortunately, Dr. Parnell and the Zigma sisters, who would often stop by in the summer to visit the house, developed a close and special bond. Indeed, Dr. Parnell subsequently became the sorority's advisor because of this experience. However, the Zigma sisters would obviously be returning to live in their house in the fall and the Parnells would once again be without a place to live.

A second closing date was set for August 30th, Mr. Seller and his attorney both swore that he would appear this time. However, at the second closing Mr. and Mrs. Seller got into a nasty fight in the settlement room and could not decide on how to escrow the proceeds from the closing. As a result, they refused a second time to provide the Parnells with a deed, even though the agreement of sale between the parties clearly listed June 30th as the time for performance. Mrs. Parnell was upset and in a desperate move, Dr. Parnell suggested that Mrs. Seller (who was living alone in the house because Mr. Seller had moved to the West Coast earlier that year) give the Parnells possession of the house at the very least and that he would pay her $1000 a month if she did so. Mrs. Seller, destitute and in need of money, accepted Parnell's offer and the parties expressed their agreement in writing (hint – we are talking about the second contract).

The Parnells were able to move before the semester began, but they did not have legal ownership. A third closing was set up for November 30th. Dr. Parnell was able to get Mr. Seller to sign the deed prior to settlement so that his attendance in the same room with Mrs. Seller would not be necessary. The third settlement went smoothly. Toward the conclusion of the settlement, after the Parnells were given the deed, Mrs. Seller politely said, "We have an outstanding issue here to discuss. The

27

Parnells never gave me a dime of my rent money for the time they lived in the house before today. They owe me $3000. I need the money. Can I have it now?" Dr. Parnell looked at Mrs. Seller directly in the eye and said, "I will give you nothing." The Parnells departed from the settlement room and headed to their home.

Challenge Questions:

1. Was there consideration to support the contract between Mrs. Seller and the Parnells for immediate possession of their house prior to closing? (Hint: we are talking about the rental agreement or second contract).

2. In your opinion, if Mrs. Seller took the Parnells to court, who would likely win?

3. In your opinion, was Dr. Parnell morally wrong to refuse to pay Mrs. Seller the $3000? (The Moral Issue).

Case 1K
The Case of Parnell Hall

Mackenzie Dolan and Lauren Dynamo had finally done it. Through hard work and the application of the many things they had learned from their favorite college professor, James Parnell, the two friends had started the world famous business "Ponies-Are-Us". From a local business specializing in the selling and leasing of ponies to children eager to become equestrians, the business had franchised its operations to become the world leader in not only the sale of ponies and horses but also (through their franchise network) "keeping and care" contracts specializing in the maintenance of horse stables. They also made large profits from giving lessons in riding and the training of the animals. With franchises open in most states and provinces in North America and a growing number of international franchises flowing royalties to the two business partners, Mackenzie and Lauren were bringing in large sums of revenues from their burgeoning business.

As their success continued they received a letter from her alma mater, Monrovia University. The college was beginning a capital campaign to finally build a state of the art academic facility, which the college intended to call "Parnell Hall". Overcome with emotion that their favorite professor would be so honored, the two women filled out charitable subscription cards and pledged a considerable sum to the building effort. Mackenzie agreed to contribute $3,000,000 to the campaign. Due to the need to support her five ex-husbands, Lauren pledged only $700,000. With the $3.7 million in pledges and the countless other smaller pledges received from Monrovia alumni, the college hired a project manager to begin the process of building the $12 million dollar Parnell Hall.

The college was pleased to receive the subscriptions. However, no money from either Mackenzie or Lauren was received. To the surprise of the women, their main global competitor had decided to put itself up for sale. The women could not pass up the opportunity to capture the lion share of the global market but to do so they needed every spare cent on which they could lay their hands. As a result, they issued no checks to Monrovia University.

Monrovia is now in a difficult position. Without the money promised by the women, it is unable to pay its project manager or contractors for the invoices submitted for the building of Parnell Hall. The vice-president of the university has consulted with you on the best course of action to deal with this serious matter.

Challenge Questions:

1. In your opinion was there consideration to support the promises of Mackenzie and Lauren to donate money to Monrovia for Parnell Hall? Further, would your opinion be different if their pledges were simply for the general fund of the college?

2. Explain how the concept of "promissory estoppel" applies to this situation. Would this concept be helpful to the college's position?

3. If you made a promise to give money to a charitable, educational or religious organization, do you think it is ethical to change your mind even if you were sure no successful lawsuit could be brought against you? (The Moral Issue).

Case 1L
Kenneth's Choice

Kenneth had enough. While he knew that both of his parents cared for him, they clearly did not like each other. His earliest memories were of the screaming, fighting, ugly words, even the pushing and shoving. As a little boy, he could not understand the reasons for it all. When Kenneth was twelve, his brother Bryan, who was six years older, left home the day after his high school graduation. Bryan would sometimes send Kenneth a postcard or a letter. Sometimes the letter even contained a small sum of money for him to use as he saw fit. He had not seen Bryan in many years and only knew that he was in the Navy, stationed in San Diego and was often at sea. When Kenneth was fifteen, his mother left the house and his father was granted sole custody of him. He learned from his cousin that his mother had several adulterous affairs and that his father had a problem with alcohol. Even though his father was the captain of police in nearby Manchester and was respected in the community, his father's problem with alcohol clearly became more acute after his wife had left him. The critical point came on Kenneth's seventeenth birthday. By that time, his mother was on her honeymoon with a stepfather that he had never met. She did not even bother to call and wish him a happy birthday. His father had little in the house to eat. Out of desperation, Kenneth went to the railroad station that linked Prince William County with the DC Metro area. At the station he was able to purchase quantities of packaged food to consume. There he spent his birthday alone. Even though he was still a junior in high school, Kenneth was determined to never go home again and to leave his past behind.

Kenneth did have some things going for him. He had a driver's license, was a hard worker, and was physically strong. Through a high school friend whose family owned a lumber business in Fredericksburg, Kenneth was able to obtain

31

employment at twice the rate of the minimum wage. He was also able to secure a small efficiency apartment about two miles from school and five miles from his job. The landlady was reluctant at first to permit him to do so, but she took pity on the handsome, polite 17-year old and thought he would be able to generate the $250 a month in rent from his thirty hours per week at the lumber yard. It was clear to Kenneth that he also needed a car.

Kenneth went down to Honest Ted Harper's lot. Honest Ted advertised that if he couldn't put you in a car, no one could. Honest Ted, through a captive finance company, also provided purchase financing for the vehicles. According to his advertisement, you only needed to come in with your driver's license and earnings statement (W-2) to qualify. Kenneth had both. With very little money in his savings account, Kenneth agreed to pay $8000 for a used Chevy Caprice. He agreed to pay the sum of $289 a month for the car over 36 months, plus an insurance payment of $50 a month. His total payment was, therefore, $339 per month. Kenneth signed the contract and a promissory note for the loan (a type of contract).

A few weeks before, Kenneth had met Kata. Ostensibly, Kata was a first year college student at Prince William County Community College. She was originally from Moldavia and had a student visa to stay in the United States. Kata, like many young eastern European women, had come to the US to work in the confectionary industry in order to escape the poverty of her native land. Although she was sixteen months older than Kenneth, they were instantly attracted to each other and soon fell madly in love. While she had a job, her work was for 35 hours a week and only paid minimum wage. Only by sharing expenses with six other women from her homeland, was she able to survive. A few days after Kenneth moved into his apartment, Kata moved in as well and was living with him. Kenneth's father did not approve of Kata or of the fact that Kenneth had moved out. While he was insistent that Kenneth return home, he was aware of his reputation in the community and didn't care to draw attention to his family problems. As a result, he did not take any court action to force Kenneth to come home.

Even with the modest addition of Kata's income, the burden of rent, food, utilities, and car payments was too much for Kenneth. After seven months, he was forced to ask his employer for an increase in hours. Now starting his senior year in high school, Kenneth was hoping for an academic scholarship so he could go on to college. He knew his grades might suffer. In addition, one late September day, after seeing Kata nauseous once again, Kata broke the news to Kenneth that at seventeen, he was soon to become a father. Kenneth had to make a choice. He couldn't and wouldn't give up his apartment. Besides, his father had made it clear that he would never permit Kata to live with them. The car had to go if Kenneth was going to make ends meet. Unfortunately there were still 29 months left on his loan payment. He went to speak to Honest Ted. Ted explained that he could return the vehicle, but that he would have to pay an outstanding loan balance of $7,300 less a $2,500 credit for the car. Kenneth simply did not have the $4,900 difference. Ted told him to "pay it or else," and to read the terms of his contract which committed Kenneth to this arrangement. At seventeen, the full weight of the world seemed to be on him. He made the choice to return the car to Ted. However, he did not give Ted any money.

Challenge Questions:

1. How does "the law of contractual capacity" apply to Kenneth's choice?

2. In your opinion, if Honest Ted took Kenneth to court, who would most likely win?

3. In your opinion, is Ted morally wrong by his insistence that Kenneth pay off the balance of his loan? (The Moral Issue).

Case 1M
A Premarital Agreement

Crete Baldwin and Jenny Creston were serious about each other. They had dated for several years in college. Both families approved of the match and the happy couple was eager to get on with their lives, buy a house, and perhaps in time, start a family themselves. When Crete proposed to Jenny he was confident that she would accept. An excellent student and intelligent person, Jenny had the good fortune to be sought after by several prospective employers. Jenny knew that Crete had been unusually successful in his business activities, which he had initiated with two of his college friends. Jenny and Crete decided the time was right, but after they had agreed to wed, things began to turn downhill.

Crete had been more successful than Jenny had realized. The stock of Delta Industries had gone public and Crete's business interests were now valued at $15 million. Crete's attorney suggested that the couple enter into a premarital agreement. Stunned by the proposal to sign such an agreement, Jenny regained her composure and asked to see a written list of potential terms and conditions before she would consider it. At Crete's' request, his attorney prepared a proposal for the following terms:

- In the event of divorce, Jenny would surrender all equitable distribution rights in any property individually titles in Crete's name. Marital property would be split 50/50.
- The couple would agree to create a "Common Monthly Expense (CME) Account" in which each individual would be allowed to keep any other money earned by them in individual accounts.
- Jenny would agree to be primarily responsible to care for any children born to the couple and to take care of all household duties and obligations for the maintenance of the family and house.
- In the event of divorce, Jenny would agree to accept the sum of $500,000 and would make no other demand for any other assets or spousal support.

Jenny did not know what to do. She loves Crete but the agreement seemed fundamentally unfair and she was uncertain of how to respond. She expressed her reservations to Crete, who replied, "Look my lawyer insists that you sign it or advises that I not get married. It is that simple and that's my call, babe." Jenny was speechless. Jenny decided to take a cruise to Jamaica to think it over.

Challenge Questions:

1. How does the "Statue of Frauds" apply to the above case?

2. In your opinion, what terms and conditions should be included in the agreement?

3. In your opinion, would you consent to enter into a premarital agreement if your spouse-to-be demanded that you do so? (The Moral Issue).

Case 1N
Monkey Man
(Based upon a true case)

Tyler Billera was always considered a nice looking young man, but Tyler had a problem. Even though he knew his girlfriend, Samantha Stout, loved him, she was obsessed with the actor Ben Affleck and would talk about her admiration for him in an open and expressive way to all who cared to listen, even to her boyfriend, Tyler. It seemed as if Tyler could never really compete with the actor in Samantha's mind, no matter what he did. Finally, things came to a head when Tyler learned that Samantha attempted to sneak into Ben Affleck's hotel room when he came to town to promote his most recent movie. She was found waiting in the actor's bed when the police arrested her. Tyler needed to do something to fight for the woman he loved.

Tyler went to a plastic surgeon. Dr. Herika Glair was known for her "radical surgery" techniques. Indeed, Dr. Glair advertised that she could even replace the skin and bone structure of your entire face to match an entertainer of your choice. Tyler went to Dr. Glair and it was agreed that for $80,000 she would perform an operation that would replace Tyler's face with one identical to Ben Affleck's. Tyler was sure that Samantha would be in love with him forever after the operation.

The first phase of the operation proceeded without problems. However, after Tyler's face was removed and discarded, Dr. Glair discovered, to her horror, that she had used her last Ben Affleck face kit and that her box of human faces was empty. Not wanting Tyler to be faceless, she opened her animal face box and used an ape kit to stitch onto Tyler. The operation was successful; at least

Tyler had a face again.

In recovery, Dr. Glair explained to Tyler what had happened. She said he would most likely get used to it and that he should learn to shave more frequently. Tyler was horrified when he looked into the mirror. How would Samantha, or any woman for that matter, react when they saw him and his grotesque appearance? Tyler wanted revenge.

Challenge Questions:

1. What remedies for breach of contract are available to Tyler?

2. How would you determine damages in this case?

3. If you were Tyler would you undergo radical surgery simply to please your partner? (The Moral Issue).

Case 10
Liquidated Damages

Carolyn O'Connell never imagined her life would ever get this depressing. She didn't want to move from her hometown of Waltham, Massachusetts to the Lehigh Valley. As one of six children and a large extended family, she felt a high level of comfort and familiarity with her native New England. Having two girls of her own now, she realized even more how important family was to her. But her husband, Conrad, had found a better paying job in Pennsylvania and Carolyn, at 34 years old, was committed to having a successful marriage.

After a month long search, Carolyn and Conrad through a local real estate agent, had found a colonial-style house for sale in a nice neighborhood in Beckham, Pennsylvania. A science professor at nearby Monrovia College owned the House. After some difficult negotiations with Dr. Culpepper, the parties came to an agreement to pay the sum of $200,000 for the house. It seemed like a high sum to Carolyn but Conrad assured her that with his new job they could afford to make the payments on the $160,000 mortgage. Putting their $40,000 in life savings down as earnest money in escrow also concerned Carolyn, but once again Conrad said it would all be okay. Dr. Culpepper was a widower and was about to retire. Culpepper insisted that his attorney, James Parnell, hold the down money in escrow. Using a standard realtor's contract, the parties agreed to use the earnest money of $40,000 as liquidated damages in the event of breach of contract. Dr. Culpepper would not agree to any other contingencies; not even a mortgage contingency.

Things seemed to be moving smoothly as the time for settlement approached. Just two weeks left and they would settle on the house and be able to move out of the crowded motel room where the family was staying. The girls, six and eight, liked the pool, but they were in school now and it was hard for the girls to explain to their new friends just why they lived in a motel. Then it happened.

Conrad was away again on one of his many business trips - to Chicago this time. Carolyn knew that Conrad did not like her to call him every night but she was lonely and didn't have any real friends yet in the Lehigh Valley. She called Conrad on Wednesday, really more out of loneliness than anything else. She then got the shock of her life. Conrad, in brutally honest terms, told Carolyn that he was sorry but he would not be returning to her. He had been having an affair with a co-worker and had fallen in love. He was taking a job in the Chicago area and wasn't coming back to Pennsylvania. His girlfriend was with him and they planned to live together. Conrad was also about to become a father for the third time. At first Carolyn was too stunned to react, and then she started to cry. Conrad told her if she was going to be a baby about it, then he was hanging up. He wasn't sure if it was a good idea for the couple to contact each other again in the near future. He did, however, want Carolyn to give his love to the girls.

When Carolyn recovered her wits, she realized that she had to return to her family, friends and support system in Massachusetts. She had no job and nothing to keep her in the Lehigh Valley. She also had no reason to own a house she couldn't afford; that was for sure. She called up both her realtor and James Parnell and explained what had happened. She wanted her life savings of $40,000 back. It was all of the money she had in the world and she would need every cent to survive. Could Parnell please send her a check?

When Parnell called Culpepper to tell him about Carolyn's hard luck, Culpepper was more annoyed than anything else. He asked Parnell if he was legally obligated to return the money. Parnell told him that he wasn't but it seemed like the right thing to do. Culpepper responded: "Tell them that their domestic problems aren't mine. And by the way, Mr. Bleeding Heart Lawyer, write me a check for $40,000. The O'Connells are in breach of contract."

Later that same month, Dr. Culpepper sold his house for $220,000 in a private transaction without a real estate agent. Not only did he make an additional $20,000 in the deal but he also saved $12,000 in real estate commissions.

Challenge Questions:

1. In your opinion, were the O'Connells in breach of contract?

2. How is the concept of liquidated damages applicable to this case? Also, how is the earnest money held in escrow connected to the concept of liquidated damages?

3. Legal issues aside, if you were Dr. Culpepper would you have returned the $40,000 to Carolyn? (The Moral Issue).

Case 1P
The Dean's Dilemma

Madison Shaman is the Dean of the College at Monrovia College. Monrovia is a small college but Madison has a big problem. Here are the facts:

- To prepare students for a changing world increasingly dependent on technology, the college in recent years made a strategic decision to start a new, innovative and flexible academic program in information systems (IS). The initiative has proven to be very successful. After just five years, the program already constitutes 14% of the student population at Monrovia and is the second largest major at Monrovia.

- While large in numbers, the IS program is short of faculty. Just three full time faculty and a revolving group of part time faculty teaching mostly at night are staffing the courses. Dean Shaman knows that the program is understaffed.

- Dr. Ted Sovoth is the Chair and a full Professor of IS. He is a highly competent and popular teacher. He is also an energetic administrator and manages to keep the program together despite the fact it is under-resourced. For his efforts, Dr. Sovoth is drawing a salary of $95,000. While his salary is above average for Monrovia faculty, it is substantially below average for professors in the IS field on a nationwide basis.

-   Dr. Sovoth is committed to teaching an overload in addition to his normal teaching and administrative responsibilities. His classes typically draw three times the number of students than the college average. As a result 180 out of a total of 1,500 undergraduates are enrolled in his classes for the fall semester.

-   Two days prior to the start of the new academic year, Dr. Sovoth informs Dean Shaman that he is leaving the college to take a faculty position at Kansas Eastern University. KEU has promised him a salary of $130,000 and a lighter teaching load. For Sovoth, it is not just a matter of money. A father of four children, Sovoth is concerned about his family as well, especially the twins, Corey and Matt. At just eight years old, little Corey has already faced criminal charges for serious felonies. Sovoth and his spouse also suspect that Matt has established ties to both organized crime syndicates and international terrorist organizations. Sovoth feels that a change is needed and a move to Kansas is just the thing.

With the new semester about to begin and the IS department in disarray, Dean Shaman does not know what to do. Dr. Sovoth signed a contractual commitment letter with Monrovia promising to work during the upcoming year. He is in breach. She calls a new young economics professor, who also has experience as an employment lawyer. The professor, James Parnell, is asked to advise the dean on this matter.

Challenge Questions:

1. What remedies exist to assist the college with this serious employment problem caused by Dr. Sovoth's breach?

2. As a college, would you prefer to bring a case against Sovoth in law or equity?

3. Contract obligations aside and considering the potential problems for the college, do you believe that Dr. Sovoth has an ethical duty to fulfill his contract to Monrovia and to give the college at least a year's notice before he departs? (The Moral Issue).

Case 1Q
Famous Esther's Auto World

It was the day for which Stefanie Kugel had waited for so many years. Her first new car! It took years of savings and struggling to pay her other bills. But working two jobs had brought her to the place where her dreams would come true - "Famous Esther's Auto World" of Mussel Bay, Pennsylvania.

Walking through the spacious car lot, Stef was bewildered by the variety and price of the cars. A salesperson (who liked to refer to himself as "Honest Will") saw that Stef needed help. He was happy to approach her. He showed Stef over a dozen different vehicles in her price range. Finally, Stef selected a brand new 2012 bright orange Tahoe as her choice. Will assured her that at $46,000 dollars, she could not have made a better decision and that it was only because his manager needed to reach a certain pre-determined sales target, that they were willing to sell the car that inexpensively to her. Stef wrote a check for $46,000, all of the money she had saved throughout her life, and left "Famous Esther's Car Lot" feeling like she was living life large. (Later, she would learn that the same automobile could be purchased at another dealership for $4,000 less).

After six days of ownership. Stef noticed that her new vehicle was making a clunking sound. She drove immediately to the dealership and asked for Will. Will listened to the auto and told her that it was a common sound that all new "Tahoes" make. She would need to drive it for another 1,000 miles or so before the sound would disappear. Stef did as Will instructed but after another month and 1,000 miles, she noticed the problem getting worse not better. She returned to Famous Esther's lot.

Will assured Stef that it was nothing serious and that he would have Tony, a crack auto mechanic, look at it. The auto was returned to Stef three days later and she was told that a slight adjustment to the drive shaft was made to correct the problem. At first all seemed well, but on her way back to work, the car sounded worse than before. Alarmed, she turned around and returned once again to Famous Esther's.

Stef was told to leave the auto for a week this time and that the dealership would thoroughly check it over. It was inconvenient for Stef to do so, but she assumed it was necessary. After a week, she was glad to get her Tahoe back; then it happened. On her way back to her apartment, the auto made the same noise; but this time the steering wheel also locked. Stef lost control of the automobile and it skidded off the side of the road just missing little Katie Nazareth who was playing nearby. The child was hysterical and her parents were soon on the scene screaming and yelling at Stef.

Stef didn't know what to do. Her dream had become a nightmare.

Challenge Questions:

1. How does the law of warranties apply to Stef's situation?

2. Are state lemon laws applicable to this situation?

3. If you were Famous Esther, what decision would you make if Stef asked you to give her all her money back? (The Moral Issue).

CHAPTER 2
AGENCY

Case 2A
A Matter of Trust

The good news was that James Parnell had passed the bar in two states and was given a job offer with a law firm in Philadelphia. The bad news was that Parnell had no employment until late October. Without any money coming in, the summer would be a long one. Leo, Parnell's second cousin, had heard of his relative's plight and had an idea. After ten years as a corporate attorney with a large financial services company, Leo had recently taken the bold move of opening up his own law office. After only six months, Leo's business was booming. Leo and his secretary were feeling the effects of being overworked. Leo asked Parnell to work part time for him in the summer to ease his load. He would pay Parnell 40% of whatever time he billed and would provide Parnell with the clients. Parnell agreed to the four-month assignment.

An acquaintance of Leo's, Alex Cantor, had also made the decision to go out on his own. Alex was a tax accountant for a large pharmaceutical company and was sick and tired of being on the road. Alex was also a resident of Northern New Jersey, but was presently on a six-month tax audit in Boston. He provided Leo with power of attorney and asked him to find an office building suitable for not only an accountant's office, but also some additional office space in order to generate the cash flow he needed to support him while he expanded his practice. Leo was busy, but took the case anyway and gave Parnell the assignment to search for a small office building per Alex's request.

At 22 years old Parnell was not experienced in real estate matters, but with the constraints given to him he diligently searched for a suitable property. He came across what seemed to be a perfect location in Upper Claremont Village. The building was 'for sale by owner' and Parnell called the number on the sign and agreed to meet the owner, 86-year-old Clive Tripplet. Upon meeting Clive, Parnell came to the conclusion that not only was Clive eccentric, but he also appeared semi-lucid. Parnell had to endure Clive's repeated comments about his hatred and mistrust of lawyers and real estate brokers. He also stated that he had purchased the building for $8,500 in 1931 and that he was firm in his price of $85,000 since he believed that the building was worth ten times what he paid for it. The building impressed Parnell. It was three stories high, ornate, well constructed, and perfectly located in the center of an affluent town. On the street level, four upscale retail stores were doing business and Parnell was sure that they were paying rents that were suitable for 30 years ago.

Parnell called a friend, Bob Delgreco, who was in the real estate business. A real estate broker at 29, Bob already had ten years experience in his family's commercial real estate business. Bob looked at the building and told Parnell "Jimmy, this building is worth from $350,000 to $400,000 at least. At the lower range I could sell the property in two weeks. Why don't you tell the guy that you are buying it for yourself, enter into a long term contract with a four month settlement date, and sell the contract by assignment before the settlement date- in our business we call that flipping the deal". Parnell considered what his broker friend had said, but instead he called Alex and told him about the great deal. Alex moved immediately and purchased that building. Alex was delighted at the results.

For his legal services, Parnell submitted a time sheet to his cousin for twenty hours of time spent on the case. His cousin, billing out at $35 per hour, sent a bill to Alex for $700. After settlement and without paying the bill, Alex asked to meet with Parnell and Leo. Alex (accountant to the end) insisted on an adjustment to the bill. "Time for meeting with the old guy, what is this? I am not paying for meetings, travel time, or telephone calls," said Alex. Leo, not wanting to fight a client, agreed to accept 60%

of the bill, or $420. Parnell was paid $168 for his work. Years later Parnell learned that Alex had sold the building for $740,000 after owning it for seven years. He also learned that Alex made over $200,000 in positive cash flow from rents in that time.

Later in life Parnell became an expert in the area of accountants' liability and to this day often acts as co-counsel in lawsuits for plaintiffs suing accountants for professional malpractice.

Challenge Questions:

1. How does "Fiduciary Duty," as it applies to agents, pertain to this fact situation?

2. In your opinion, would Parnell have breached that duty if he took advantage of this investment opportunity?

3. In your opinion, (especially given the attitude of the client) would you have taken the chance of violating your legal duty and 'flipping the deal'? (The Moral Issue).

Case 2B
Buying the Magic Kingdom

The seat of Orange County, Orlando was known as a regional center for commerce in the heavily agricultural area of Central Florida. The area south of the town consisted of mostly citrus fruit farms and small towns serving the local farm population. Contrary to belief, Orange County was substantially above sea level and while several rivers ran through the county, there was very little swampland in it. With its year round warm weather and ample land, the area south of Orlando seemed to be the perfect place to build Walt Disney's dream, the largest entertainment park in the history of humankind. Disney's thoughts were grandiose. To realize his dreams he decided to purchase a tract of land, which exceeded 47 square miles (twice the size of the island of Manhattan), over 30,000 acres of land. How would he purchase this vast tract of land without bankrupting his company?

The idea was to purchase the land cheap from the farmers, dedicate about 1,100 acres of it to the several parks he had planned, and sell small tracts of the remaining land over time to commercial developers who wished to build hotels, restaurants, and other enterprises catering to the many expected tourists. Disney figured the mark up of the land in the first ten years of development could easily exceed $20,000 per acre from its initial cost. In other words, purchase land for as low $80 an acre and sell it for $25,000 or more an acre. Farmland was selling for a little less than $100 an acre in that part of Orange County. Disney first set up a group of dummy corporations with names like M.T. Lott Corporation (get it – empty lot) and Reedy Ranch Corporation. He then contracted with a small group of energetic real estate brokers and made them swear an oath that under no circumstances would they reveal the fact that they were operating as agents for the Disney Corporation. Disney agreed to pay them a generous commission for every purchase. With hundreds of thousands of dollars of potential commissions, the agents were happy to agree to work for Disney. They knew that they stood to forfeit every last dollar if they told anyone about the agreement.

The agents went into the field and contacted each landowner. They did not tell the farmers for whom they were buying the land. Routinely, the agents sometimes offered the farmers premiums of 20% to 50% above the market value of their land. The agents even purchased a large tract owned by a Florida state senator. Farming was a tough business and within a few years, almost all the farmers sold out to Disney's agents. Not one farmer knew that the agents were representing Disney. The agents had done their jobs well and had been paid handsomely for it.

At the conclusion of the purchase, Mickey Mouse finally revealed himself to the Orange community and told the world about his plans. Many of the farmers and their families felt violated. They had sold their land for a fraction of the price that they would have gotten if they had known that it was Disney who was purchasing the property. Indeed, some of the farmers were descendants of people in bondage who had acquired the land after the Civil War. Farming was a hard life but an honest one, and it had permitted generations of farmers the ability to independently support themselves and their families. Now what would their descendants do? Many in the Orlando community felt a sense of outrage at Disney and some civic groups complained that Disney had engaged in reputedly unethical business practices.

Challenge Questions:

1. Explain why Disney acted through "Agents for an Undisclosed Principal" to purchase the property?

2. In your opinion, did Disney act in an unethical way and destroy a way of life by its business practices in this case? (The Moral Issue).

Case 2C
Who Pays the Shrink?

It was the day that Hanna dreaded, graduation day. Unlike most of her fellow students, her parents would not be there to celebrate the occasion. Her mother had passed away during her sophomore year in college. Her father and mother had divorced when she was in high school. Her father was remarried and living in Arizona and seemed to want nothing to do with Hanna or her older sister. At least she had Shane and his family with whom to share the day. Hanna and Shane had dated since they were freshmen and had been going steady since their second year. Shane had mentioned that he needed to speak to Hanna after the ceremony was concluded, and that he had something very important to say to her. Hanna wondered if a proposal of marriage was likely, it seemed to be the logical next step. There did seem to be an air of mystery to it all since Shane had mentioned nothing about his family's dinner plans after the ceremony concluded. Something big sure was up.

As the final graduation line began to disband, Hanna could see Shane in the distance walking toward her. She was taking a picture with her sorority sisters from the Zigma sorority when Shane approached. "I need to speak with you alone" said Shane. He continued "This is hard for me to say, but the whole time we were dating in college, I had a girlfriend back in my hometown of Springfield. Anyway, we are getting married this summer and I thought I should tell you. Well, it was nice to know you, Hanna, goodbye". Shane walked away and Hanna was in shock.

Hanna didn't know what to do. The economy was bad and the job market for a college graduate was worse. She had to leave the Zigma house and find a place to live, but where? She had no home in which to dwell. She finally landed a job as a server at Peachtree Grill, a large national franchise. Fortunately, a few of her Zigma sisters invited her to room with them in their new apartment in Beckham. Her aunt on her maternal side, Genna, was worried about Hanna. Hanna seemed to be crying a lot and was always sad when they saw each other. Genna had her own family and life, but since her sister's death, she felt a motherly bond toward the somewhat lost Hanna. Genna called Hanna and asked her to lunch. "Hanna, I am so worried about you, you seem so depressed. I think you need some help". Hanna replied to her aunt "What do you think I should do, I am so confused and down these days." Aunt Genna said "I have an appointment for you with Dr. Murray Gelden, he is an excellent psychiatrist, and I think he can help you." "Okay" Hanna replied, "When do I go see him?" Her aunt told her the appointment was at 10 am on Saturday morning.

Hanna's feelings toward Dr. Gelden were mixed. He seemed nice enough but never said much and was a bit distant, as if he had other things on his mind. After three sessions, she had decided that she was getting nowhere and that the sessions were a waste of time. She cancelled her future appointments. Three weeks later as she was checking her mail, Hannah received a bill for $750 from Dr. Gelden. Calmly, she placed the bill in an envelope and sent it to her aunt with a note requesting her to pay it. A few days later she received a telephone call from her aunt. "Hanna, you cannot be serious, you were the one who received Dr. Gelden's care, not me. I am not going to pay it, you are!" Hanna was speechless; didn't her aunt know that she had no money? Besides, it was her aunt's idea all along. She refused to pay and her aunt refused to pay.

After three months of nonpayment, Dr. Gelden filed a lawsuit for the unpaid bill plus court costs and attorney fees, $1,000 overall, against Hanna. Now really depressed she turned to the one person in the world that she knew she could always trust, James Parnell, the faculty advisor to the Zigma sorority.

Challenge Questions:

1. In your opinion, who is liable to Dr. Gelden for the unpaid bill?

2. How does the doctrine of "Agency by Necessity" apply to this case?

3. As her aunt and close family member, do you think that Aunt Genna has an ethical duty to pay the bill? (The Moral Question).

Case 2D
Scope of Employment

Hal Bombari was tired. He had been fixing dryers, washing machines and refrigerators since 8 am. It was now 3:15 pm and his shift was over at 4:30 pm. As he drove east from Emmaus toward the Sears facility used as a central service area near the airport, he called his dispatcher and prayed that he not be sent on another service call. To his dismay, the dispatcher told him to head to Percy Lane in Beckham. A Kenmore stove still under warranty needed repair. Hal knew it was useless to complain.

As Hal drove to Beckham, he thought a lot about his life. At 22, he was working, supporting himself, and living on his own and going to college at night at Monrovia College. Often he would observe the traditional day students at Monrovia and wished he had their carefree life. Playing football, going to parties and attending classes in the day, that was the life. Instead he had to go and fix some idiot's stove. What an unfair world!

At Percy Lane, Stephanie Praterous was waiting. It had been a bad day. Her three-year-old daughter was sick with a high fever. She knew it was an ear infection and the doctor had called in a prescription. She had tried to heat up some soup for her little girl but her stovetop would not work. She had separated from husband over a year ago. He was not sending the children support payments with the regularity he had promised and she was beginning to have some serious financial problems. She was glad when Hal arrived. Hal quickly diagnosed the problem with the stove. The burners had to be replaced and he had several kits in his van that would easily fit. Hal explained to Stephanie what to do if it happened again.

There was something about Hal that Stephanie liked. Or maybe she was just lonely, who knew? As Hal completed his work and began to pack up his toolbox, Stephanie asked him if he would like to have an iced tea before he left. Hal usually made it a point to never accept food or beverages from customers. However, there was something about Stephanie's soft sad smile and pretty brown eyes that made him change his mind.

The next morning when Hal woke up, Stephanie asked him why he had to go so early. Hal told her it was a workday and he was already running late. Hal quickly washed up and dressed. He walked to his repair truck and got on the radio to contact his dispatcher. The dispatcher told him to head to a residential neighborhood in Salisbury Township; there was a refrigerator in need of repair. Another day was about to begin. As Hal backed the van out of Stephanie's driveway he heard a thud. Little Antonio, a ten-year-old newspaper delivery boy, was finishing his morning run and riding his bike home. Hal never saw him. Hal stopped the van and checked on Antonio, the boy was hurt and his leg had been shattered. Hal called an ambulance. He was relieved to learn that although Antonio was badly hurt, doctors were confident that he would make a full recovery. On behalf of Antonio, a lawsuit was filed against Sears and Hal in tort for damagers in excess of $50,000. Sears, through its attorneys, claimed that Hal was "On Frolic of his Own" and, therefore, Sears was not civilly liable for his actions.

Challenge Questions:

1. When Hal ran over Antonio was he acting within the scope of his employment? In other words, was Sears civilly liable under the "Doctrine of Respondeat Superior" for the action of its employee, Hal?

2. In your opinion should Hal be fired for his "frolic" in this case? (The Moral Question).

CHAPTER 3
EMPLOYMENT LAW

Case 3A
Family Insecurity

Even though he was 25 years older than her, Baldy Ewell was the love of Jaclyn Banic-Ewell's life. Together, they had a daughter, Brittani, who the couple affectionately called "Little Baldy". Then it happened. The happy couple was driving back from their 15th anniversary party when a Mercedes-Benz driven by Noah Tuttle, crossed over the median barrier and crashed into them. Baldy died instantly and Jaclyn was disabled by the accident. Luckily, their 4-year-old daughter, Brittani, was at home with a babysitter at the time. While she would slowly recover from her injuries, the doctors told Jaclyn that she would never be able to work again at her job as a supervisor of a large commercial office building. The uninsured and bankrupt Noah was sent to prison for negligent homicide and for driving while intoxicated.

With the death of her husband and loss of her job, Jaclyn was without health insurance and a steady income. The Ewell family was well off, but the patron of the family, Corman Ewell, refused to share any of the family's wealth with Jaclyn. As she sat in her room at home trying to recover from the injury, Jaclyn worried; how would she take care of herself and Little Baldy?

Challenge Questions:

1. Explain how the system created by the social security law might help Jaclyn in this situation?

2. If your cousin became disabled, would you expend your own funds or those of your family trust to assist them? (The Moral Issue).

Case Exercise 3B
Time to Choose

You have recently graduated from Monrovia College. You receive a job offer at an international distribution corporation in the collections and receivables department. Your starting gross salary is $36,000 per year. You have made a decision that with rent, food, household expenses and car-related costs that you will need about $2,000 a month just to cover your basic needs. Your company offers a number of free benefits and optional benefits. You will also have to worry about payroll deductions for income taxes and mandatory benefits. Here is what you need to think about:

A. Taxes

    1.   Taxes for Income, etc.
- Federal (10% minimum)
- State   (3.1%)
- Local   (1.0%)
- Other Taxes (About $8 per month)

    2.   Taxes for Mandatory Benefits
- Social Security (6.20%)
- Medicare   (1.45%)

B. Benefits

    3. Company Paid Benefits
- Health Insurance (Company pays entire premium)
- Life Insurance (Company pays entire premium for 1x Salary)
- Defined Contribution Plan (Company matches up to 5%)
- Dependent Care Reimbursement (up to $3,000 a year)
- Tuition Assistance (up to $1,500 a year)

    4. Optional Benefits
- Medical Reimbursement (up to $2,500 per year)
- Additional Life Insurance ($17 per $1,000 up to age 25)
- Long Term Care Insurance ($22 per $1,000 up to age 25)
- Disability Insurance ($8 per $1,000 up to age 25, for 50% LT)
- Accident Insurance ($11 per $1,000 up to age 25)

Challenge Questions:

1. Meeting with your group, make decisions on how to divide your salary? Which benefits would you choose and which would you forego? Explain your answer.

2. You calculate that you could save about $1,000 a month on rent and food if you live with your parents, is it worth it?

3. Do you believe that your new employer has a moral duty to pay for all of the benefits listed above or is the breakdown listed fair? (The Moral Issue).

Case 3C
The Van

Eugene and Maggie Kulick finally reached their goal. Through hard work, overtime, Maggie's part time job, and the money their teenagers contributed, they had saved the $5,000 they needed for a down payment on a house with just enough money left over for the closing fees. With the promise of a VA loan, Eugene was able to sign a real estate sales agreement for the purchase of a small house in a crime-free neighborhood. The Kulicks did not, however, have any cash to spare. They knew they would have to economize on the move.

Sometimes Eugene really missed his time in the navy. But he met Maggie, he married, had four children and navy life was not compatible with family life. After the navy, Eugene had difficulty finding and keeping a job. He was a hard worker but had limited skills. Finally, he landed a position as a line cook at Gordon's Food Products, Inc., a regional baker and food processing company. The job did not pay a lot, but the work was steady and Eugene was well liked by his fellow employees and often would intervene on their behalf in the non-union company. As Eugene contemplated moving his family's belongings from their apartment to their new home, one of his friends at work, Tony Costelos, suggested that he borrow the company's van. During the week, the company used the van to make direct deliveries to smaller customers. On the weekend the van just sat in the parking lot behind the loading dock at the company's facility. Tony told Eugene that he was responsible for the keys and that he would make sure that the keys were available on a hook outside his workspace. And if the keys were taken by someone else and returned before Monday morning, who would know? Eugene saw a way to save $100 and did not want to pass it up.

On Saturday morning, Eugene and his 16-year old son drove to the plant. The keys were in the place promised by Tony. With the help of his family and a few friends, Eugene managed to move his meager property to the new house with the help of the company van. Eugene was careful to thoroughly clean the van, outside and inside, before he returned it. He also made sure that the gas tank was filled prior to its return.

During the following week, word filtered through the plant about Eugene's use of the van. This information circulated up to Ed Higgins, the general manager of the Montgomery County Plant where Eugene worked. Upon learning about Eugene's use of the company property, Ed called Eugene into his office, and on the spot fired him. Ed told Eugene that he was not dissatisfied with his work, but could not permit employees to use company property that way and besides, there were liability issues to consider.

Eugene filed for unemployment insurance. Concerned about its experience ratings, Gordons filed forms opposing Eugene's claim. In its opposition filing, Gordons stated that Eugene was fired for misuse of company property. With a new house, four kids and other responsibilities, Eugene needed that unemployment insurance money to survive. Through a friend, he had heard of an attorney named James Parnell. He called Parnell and asked for his assistance. His father in law offered to pay part of his attorney's fees.

Challenge Questions:

1. Taking the company's side, what is the best argument it can make to deny Eugene unemployment compensation under the law?

2. Taking Eugene's side, what is the best argument he or his attorney can make to obtain benefits for Eugene?

3. Do you think that the company was correct in firing Eugene in this case? (The Moral Issue).

Case 3D
In Re Andrea Pilson

Andrea Pilson had it tough. She was a single mom, and her husband had left the family years earlier and had never paid alimony or support to either Andrea or her three children. The last information Andrea had about him was a rumor that he was serving time for armed robbery in Indiana. She did not, however, know if this information was correct. To support her and the kids (ages 3 to 8) Andrea worked at Amalgamated Chemical, Inc, (ACI) a large multi-national corporation. The work was hard, sometimes dangerous but the pay was decent and with her salary, Andrea was just about able to make ends meet. Kids being kids, infections, illnesses and other childhood ailments often went through the family. As a result of these illnesses and school closings, Andrea was often late to work and called in sick at a rate twice that of the average at ACI. ACI did not have a corporate sponsored day care center.

Upon reviewing personnel records, the general manager at the Conshohocken plant, decided that Andrea's tardiness and absences had exceeded written company work rules. She was issued a termination warning. The warning stated that if she violated the rules one more time, she would be fired. For the next two months, Andrea struggled to get to work and come on time. However, one morning her youngest child went into convulsions from a high fever and Andrea rushed her to the hospital. By the time the baby's condition was stabilized, she was three hours late for work. When she showed up to ACI later that day, she was fired.

Andrea filed for unemployment compensation with the PA Bureau of Employment Security. The company opposed the claim stating that she had willfully and wantonly violated a company work rule. The bureau agreed with the company and Andrea's claim was denied. The claim was for $300 per week in unemployment benefits. Andrea filled out the appeal papers and appeared before an unemployment-hearing officer (known as a referee). She was unaware that she had a right to be represented by counsel. The company through its attorney and managers brought her personnel file and attendance records. Andrea claimed that she had permission from her supervisor, Ryan Cohlbecker, for each and every late day or missed day. She did not, however, ask Ryan to appear at the hearing in order to testify on her behalf and the company objected to her testimony as hearsay evidence. The referee sustained the objection and dismissed her claim. Finally, Andrea went to Community Legal Services of Delaware County and asked for their representation and assistance in her claim. CLS requested a judicial review of the case before the PA Commonwealth Court. The attorney assigned to the appeal to assist Andrea received the case 17 months after Andrea was fired. According to the file, Andrea was living on only $220 a month of social welfare benefits. The attorney, 23-year-old James Parnell, could not understand how Andrea was even surviving. Having just inherited the case from a departing attorney, he called her up to ask her to come into the office for a case update.

With all of the stress in her life, Parnell expected to see a 30-year-old woman who looked like she was 60. To his surprise, Andrea was fit and very attractive. She was wearing expensive jewelry and had driven to the office in a brand new luxury automobile. She was clearly intelligent and understood the aspects of the case for the $8,000 in back compensation. When she left, Parnell was puzzled. How was it that Andrea was able to afford such expensive items of property and why did she seem so prosperous? As he was pondering the question, the firm's investigator came into his office and said, "Was that Andrea who just came in here?" Parnell responded in the affirmative. Jokingly, the investigator said "How can you afford $600 per hour on your salary here"? At that moment, the mystery became clear for Parnell.

Challenge Questions:

1. Identify the administrative law issues in this case.

2. In your opinion, which side should win this case and why do you have that opinion?

3. To be eligible to receive unemployment compensation, the claimant must be without "earned income". In your opinion, is Parnell wrong to represent Andrea in her claim before the court? (The Moral Issue).

Case 3E
Chelsea Feels Tired

Dr. Kelsey Lashworth, superintendent of the Claremont School District, has a problem. The Principal of the Claremont Middle School, Brendan Anieda, has told Dr. Lashworth that one of his teachers, Chelsea Lortz, has made an ADA (Americans with Disability) request for reduced hours at full pay and benefits. Chelsea claims that she suffers from chronic fatigue syndrome (CFS). To accommodate her disability Chelsea has made the following demands to her Principal:

- That she not be required to teach more than two class periods in a row. (There are six class periods during a normal school day).

- That she be given at least three breaks during the school day to rest on the sofa in the teachers' lounge or, in the alternative, be permitted to take a two hour lunch break to go to her home and rest.

- That she be excused from all extra-curricular activities.

Superintendent Lashworth is concerned. She feels that if accommodates Chelsea she will only be able to perform half of what is expected of her. She will have to obtain a replacement for work that she will not do. In addition Lashworth is also worried that other teachers will seek to emulate Chelsea's example. Dr. Lashworth calls the district's solicitor. The law firm representing the district dispatches James Parnell to advise the superintendent. Parnell tells Dr. Lashworth that CFS has never been recognized by a court of law as a physical disability. Further, emotional and psychological illnesses are listed by the EEOC as disabilities but only in its "interpretative rules".

Challenge Questions:

1. Are the EEOC's interpretative rules binding on the district?

2. In your opinion, should Dr. Lashworth accede to Chelsea's demands?

3. Do you believe that the district would be morally right to fire Chelsea if she refused to fully meet the commitments expected of a full time teacher? (The Moral Issue).

Case 3F
Griggs v Duke Power Company

Earl "Chuck" Clarkson was born in Illinois. He lived there most of his life until he went to college. After college and graduate school, Earl worked his way up the managerial ranks in the public utility industry. At age 47, he received an offer to become the President of Duke Power Company, one of the largest electric utilities in the South. Duke Power's service area included half of Middle and Western Virginia, Eastern Tennessee, and Northern Georgia. It was big.

A progressive Midwesterner in the mostly rural South, Earl was determined to change the past discriminatory policies of Duke. Indeed, in the past, Duke had segregated its work force to such an extent that only African-Americans were hired to work in the coal yards and in the maintenance departments. Of course, the down side was that African-American employees rarely were able to obtain employment in other, more lucrative positions in the company. Earl not only used his CEO position to end these clearly discriminatory practices, he went one step further.

In order to place all employees on a more equal footing Earl decided that all Duke employees without exception must:

- Have a high school diploma or equivalent. Those present employees without a diploma would be given paid time off and financial assistance to obtain one.

- Achieve a minimum score on an entry aptitude test.

Earl was determined that only educated, capable people were going to work at Duke from now on, it did not matter if they were white or black.

Even though Earl Clarkson had ended the institutionalized approach to job segregation at Duke, the African-American employees were far from happy. They resented the fact that they were now obligated to obtain diplomas and minimum test scores simply to keep their jobs. How did the ability to quote Shakespeare help them when they were shoveling coal? A group of African-American employees sued Duke Power, claiming that the new company policies resulted in unlawful discrimination under Title 7 of the 1964 Civil Rights Act.

Many legal scholars see the Griggs case as one of the ten most influential decisions ever rendered by the U.S. Supreme Court.

Challenge Questions:

1. Explain the notion of disparate or unequal impact? How does it differ from the bases known as "overt discrimination" or "differential or unequal treatment"?

2. In your opinion, did Earl Clarkson do the ethical thing in his attempt to reform Duke Power Company or was he simply unable to understand the depth of cultural discrimination in the South and the effects that his policies would have on working people? (The Moral Issue).

CHAPTER 4
BUSINESS ORGANIZATIONS AND CORPORATIONS

Case 4A
ABC Printing Company
(Another Sad but True Story)

After meeting at a "poker" night party, Bert told Charlie about a man he met who worked as a plumber's assistant named Adam. Adam had spent most his life as a printer and was looking for people with business skills and capital who might want to start up a printing company. Bert knew how hard it was to find a reliable printer in the Northern New Jersey area. Whenever there was a wedding or baptism in his family, he found it difficult to get the printed invitations he needed. Adam bragged about how much experience he had as a master printer and Bert was sure that the guy knew everything there was to know about the printing trade. Charlie owned a small venture capital boutique. His firm consisted of him and a part-time secretary. He had inherited $5,000,000 at the time of his father's death and most of the money invested by the firm was his own. Although he was 36 years old, Charlie still lived at home with his mother in Convent Station, New Jersey. Charlie liked to say that he helped take care of her, but in reality his mother was physically fit and usually looked after him. Charlie considered himself a skillful and experienced investor. Even though two out of three ventures failed, the one time they would hit would produce spectacular profits for him and over time he had managed to increase his fortune as a result. Besides, what else was he going to do?

Adam, Bert, and Charlie met and decided to form the ABC Printing Company. They would capitalize the business at $60,000, each party was obligated to put up $20,000 and they would become co-equal partners. The problem was that Adam had no money, so Bert and Charlie agreed to lend him his share and Adam agreed to pay them back out of his share of the profits. Adam, being the only full time employee of the company, would also draw a small salary and he would try to operate the business with five or six part time employees. The partners found a vacant warehouse in Newark, New Jersey, to use for their printing business. The city's economic development agency gave them a lease on the facility at a very low monthly rate. Adam was able to locate some used printing equipment. The rest of the capital was applied to the purchase of supplies and office furniture and to advertise the opening of the business. After only eight months of doing business the partnership was already making a profit and the company's bank account had $12,000 in it. With no debt and sales increasing, things looked up for ABC Printing. Then it happened.

Slick Simon was a salesperson for Hartwell Corporation, a large producer of business machinery. Slick made a sales call on ABC and had a glossy brochure of a new model-printing machine referred to as "The Super Deluxe Line" (Model SDL) printer. The Model SDL could do everything and do it quicker and more efficiently than any other printer that ever existed. Adam was sold. As a Master Printer with 40 years of experience, he knew that the Model SDL would revolutionize the industry. But there was a problem. At $160,000, the machine cost too much. Slick said there was no problem. Hartwell had a financing plan that allowed the firm to buy the machine with no money down and 36 months to pay at 18% interest. Problem solved. Adam signed the contract of purchase along with an installment sales note for $160,000. The machine was delivered within ten days.

Four months later, Bert was making his twice a month stop at the facility to inspect the books. He noticed there was two overdue notices from Honeywell for invoices totaling $10,000. He asked Adam to come into the office. Adam knew what it was about. He explained the whole Hartwell deal to Bert and tried to justify the purchase. Adam also explained to Bert that the machine was so powerful that it could not be connected or used until more electrical wattage was added to the facility and that the job might be expensive since new wiring and electrical boxes would be necessary. Bert stated "Are you crazy - we can't afford this machine!" Call Hartwell and tell them to take it back." Hartwell showed up with a truck and repossessed the machine. They sent a final invoice to ABC Printing for $125,000 broken down as follows: $80,000 for depreciation; $20,000 in back P&I payments; and $25,000 in attorneys' fees per the note. Hartwell also filed a confession of judgment for that amount in court against ABC Printing Company.

If it liquidated all of its assets, the partnership still only had $30,000 to pay the judgment. How would they come up with the remaining $95,000? Adam had no money at all. He lived in a small rented apartment and his only asset was a very used pick up truck. Adam was calm and confident he could find another job. Trying to stop the rot, Charlie paid back the entire $95,000 balance and called his attorney, a friend from his college days, James Parnell. Parnell on Charlie's behalf filed a contribution lawsuit against Adam and Bert requesting that they pay 2/3 of the judgment. Because he was destitute, the suit was functionally against Bert alone. Bert did not defend and permitted Parnell to file a judgment in court against him. Desperate, Bert called Parnell and begged him to accept a payment plan for his share whereby he would agree to pay $200 a month for the next twenty years. Parnell refused to accept the offer and filed a writ of execution and levy against Bert's assets. Execution was ordered against Bert's automobiles, household furniture, appliances, and other household goods. Two county deputy sheriffs were sent to seize the personal property and bring it to the warehouse to wait for the day of judicial sale. As the deputies approached the house, Bert's wife, Trina, with her two daughters (seven and five), was about to leave for ballet lessons. Trina seeing the deputies asked them what was wrong. The deputies informed her that they were there to seize her furniture and cars. "But officers" Trina exclaimed, "How will I get my daughters to ballet lessons if you do that?" The deputies realizing that Trina was in shock went into her house and called Parnell. "Mr. Parnell, this poor woman doesn't know anything about the execution or the case for that matter, what should we do?" Parnell replied, "Take it all, immediately!"

The property was sold and the judgment partially paid to Charlie as a result of Parnell's actions. Trina took the girls, left Bert and moved in with her parents. They are presently divorced.

Challenge Questions:

1. Explain how the concept of "mutual agency" applies to partnership?

2. What are the consequences of joint liability for general partners of a business?

3. If you had Charlie's financial resources, would you have borne the whole loss and not brought a contribution case against Bert? Further, do you think that Trina was morally justified to separate from Bert? (The Moral Issue).

Case 4B
Concurrent Property

Alice and Becky were best friends. As members of the faculty at Mulehengate College, they instantly bonded, even though they were ten years apart in age. When Becky's husband passed away, Alice was with her and Becky's children during the entire period. A single mother now of three children, Becky found it increasingly difficult to support herself and the children on an assistant professor's salary, but she did so desperately want to have a nice place to live. Alice had the solution. Alice had seen a beautiful house for sale near the edge of campus. The neighborhood and location were great but the house was too expensive for her to purchase alone. What if she and Becky pooled their money and bought the house together? Becky was thrilled at the idea. The two friends signed an agreement of the sale and applied for a mortgage. They then called a skillful attorney named James Parnell to represent them in the closing.

Parnell explained to Alice and Becky that they had two choices when it came to concurrent ownership. They could elect to be treated as "Tenants in Common". This form of ownership recognized a divisible form of ownership and either party could alienate their interest in the real estate. The other choice was to take the deed as "Joint Tenants" with the right of survivorship (JTWROS). Such a form of ownership would treat the friends as if they were married and give to them an indivisible interest, which could not be transferred even at death. The friends, wanting the house for life and believing in the durability of friendship, chose the JTWROS approach.

Five years after the transaction (Becky was then 47) Becky learned that she had a terminal disease. Alice was 57 at that time.

Despite a heroic effort at recovery, Becky knew the end was upon her. She called Parnell and asked him to meet her at the hospital to prepare her last will and testament. In that will, she left all of her earthly possessions to her three children - Denise, Elizabeth, and Frieda. All of her children were students at Penn State University at the time. Denise was a graduate student. Five days later, Becky passed away.

At the reading of the will, Parnell explained that their mother's estate consisted of a $30,000 death benefit from her pension, some household goods and $4,000 in bank deposits. After attorneys' fee and probate costs, each child would receive about $8,500 each. Elizabeth exclaimed, "what about the house? It must be worth at least $340,000. Half of it belonged to mom, we want our share!" Parnell tried to explain the different forms of concurrent ownership but the children were not satisfied with his explanation. Parnell told them that it was up to Alice to decide what to do about the house. She owned it all.

The sisters went to meet with Alice. It wasn't long before Elizabeth lost her temper again and accused Alice of stealing her mother's share of the house. The girls also used harsh and insulting language at Alice during the meeting. Alice left the house visibly upset and called Parnell. "Am I legally obligated to let the girls continue to live here during the summer or other breaks?" Parnell answered no. "Then send them each a letter giving them one week to get their things out of my house!" Parnell complied with his client's request.

Challenge Questions:

1. How would the results of this case be different if Alice and Becky chose the "Tenants in Common" approach to concurrent property?

2. To what form of concurrent ownership (co-tenancy or joint tenancy) does "Tenancy by Partnership "bear a closer resemblance?

3. If you were Alice (considering that the sisters were orphans and vulnerable at the time of Becky's death) would you give the sisters a generous cash payment to recognize their mother's interest in the house? (The Moral Issue).

Case Exercise 4C
The ABJ Automobile Dealership, GP

The ABJ Automobile Dealership is a general partnership organized under the Pennsylvania Uniform Partnership Act. The dealership has written articles of partnership. The three partners (Al, Bill, and John) were brothers. Their father, Frank, started the business. Al is 61 years old and Bill is 56. John was 57 when he passed away. Under the articles of partnership, the heirs of John have the right to the value of John's equity in the partnership at the time of his death. Under his last will John left everything to his wife. The brothers are co-equal owners of the partnership.

Here is the problem. John was married for 26 years to his college sweetheart, Simmie. Simmie and John had two children from the marriage, Xavier and Yolanda. Uncles Al and Bill are very close to their niece and nephew and were also very fond of Simmie, who is generally well liked. At age 49, John left Simmie for a considerably younger woman whom he subsequently married. John's second wife (and heir of his will), Desiree, was only 27 when they wed. From that marriage a son, Abbot, was produced. Abbot was 7 at the time of his father's death. Xavier and Yolanda are both college students. Al and Bill never liked Desiree. Partially, it was because of their warm feelings toward Simmie, and partially, because of their belief that Desiree was a gold digger after John's money. Desiree does not work and never has except for a brief engagement as a lounge singer and cocktail waitress at the Green Onion, a low class bar outside of town. Nor have the brothers been particularly close to Abbot. Despite their negative feelings for Desiree, Al and Bill remained close to their brother John until his death and were genuinely sad by his passing.

At the time of the funeral, Al and Bill approached Desiree. They told her that although they were never close to her, because of their feelings for their brother, they wished to provide her with John's share of the business valued on a net asset basis at $416,667. They also provided Desiree with a check for that amount, a release and a balance sheet provided by the company's accountants. They asked her to sign a release. She politely thanked them for their thoughtfulness but refused to either accept the check or sign the release. The next day she consulted with an attorney who advised her to seek arbitration under the articles of partnership in order to determine the true value of the business. The arbitrator appointed by the American Arbitration Association (AAA) is an experienced one. His background is that of an attorney at a prestigious law firm and a Ph.D. He is also a professor at a small but very good liberal arts college in Beckham, PA. The arbitrator is left with the task of deterring the value of the business. The business had historically been quite profitable and in addition to a small salary received by each, the brothers usually shared profits equally to the amount of $270,000 to $360,000 a year over the last five years.

You can find other financial information at the end of this case.

Challenge Questions:

1. As arbitrator, how would you determine the value of this business?

2. If the situation arose, would you take advantage of your sister-in-law or another relative when it comes to business valuation issues? (The Moral Issue).

Financial Information for Case Exercise 4C

Assets

Cash and Checking Accounts	$ 150,000
Accounts Receivable	$ 350,000
Marketable Securities	$ 270,000
Property and Equipment	$ 860,000
Real Estate (at cost less depreciation)	$ 240,000
Other Assets	$ 30,000

Total Assets   **$1,900,000**

Liabilities

Accounts Payable	$ 210,000
Notes Payable	$ 400,000
Other Liabilities	$ 40,000

Total Liabilities   **$ 650,000**

Total Liabilities and Net Worth   **$1,900,000**

Case 4D
Secession in South Carolina

At least half of the permanent residents were originally from Northern and Midwestern states. The vast majority were retirees who came to the South Myrtle Beach area for the mild climate. Briarwood was a large residential development, right along the ocean. The developer had exclusively built single-family homes pursuant to the plan of development approved by the city of South Myrtle Beach. The homes were not ostentatious but they were nice enough and the residents enjoyed a high quality of life in their neighborhood between the King's Highway and the Atlantic Ocean. Then it happened.

The Developer still had 1/3 of the land left. He asked the city planning commission for a variance from the plan to rezone the property from single-family use to multiple uses. In other words, condos! When the residents of Briarwood found out about this sinister turn of events, they mobilized into a potent force. But the director of city planning (for whatever reason) stated his support for the variance and it seemed a certainty. Usually a placid group, the residents of Briarwood could adjust to hurricanes, political instability or even Russian invasion. But condos in Briarwood! Never! The only option seemed to be secession from South Myrtle Beach. In other words, form their own municipal incorporated community; namely the Town of Briarwood. When the articles of incorporation were submitted along with the proper petition to the state, South Carolina's response was positive. "Secession, sure we are fine with that down here" and so the state issued the charter. Briarwood was now a self-governing incorporated community.

At first, all was joy with the residents. But that soon changed. Most of the town's population was above the age of 65. Being a relatively prosperous place, the former development was a ripe target for burglars. One night Ida Gorman awoke to the hushed sound of people talking. She cautiously looked out her bedroom doorway to see two large men stealing her silver. Ida quickly went into her closet bringing her telephone with her and called the South Myrtle Beach police. "There are burglars in my house, please come and help me, here is my address" said Ida. The police dispatcher responded "Look Madam we no longer have jurisdiction in Briarwood, you will have to call the state police in Conway, South Carolina." "But that is over 40 miles from me; they wouldn't able to get here for hours". "Well" said the dispatcher, "I would suggest that you learn to get along with the burglars then, there is nothing we can do." Click.

Storms were not uncommon either along coastal Carolina. The residents did not worry too much. The roads washed out but they were mostly tabby shell roads and were easily repaired. Again, after a bad storm, the residents called the South Myrtle Beach Roads Department and after he got through laughing, the roads manager told them where to go. Briarwood was no longer his responsibility. And the part-time town clerk, who set up a shop with all of the town records in a three-sided house by the ocean, was complaining that the open side faced the ocean and she and the records were getting wet. The town was going to have to raise taxes to build a real town hall.

Faced with the prospect of a massive tax increase on residents who were mostly on fixed incomes was not pleasing to the town elders. Instead they decided to form committees of residents who would be responsible for different municipal functions. There were several problems with this approach however. As they were about to celebrate their one-year anniversary as a separate municipal entity, many residents wondered; was it worth it?

At least there were no condos!

Challenge Questions:

1. Explain the process by which a geographical area becomes a municipal corporation. What rights does a municipal corporation have as a local governmental unit?

2. The residents clearly were trying to keep condos out so that they might maintain the well-to-do nature of the community. Do you think that it is fair that wealthy communities use their right of municipal governance to exclude poorer people? (The Moral Issue)

Case 4E
A Historic LBO

As soon as he got his license, Brian would drive his friends to the foundry. After all, the foundry had been in the family since 1708 and was the oldest family owned business in America. There was much of which to be proud. Indeed during his retreat from Long Island to New Jersey, George Washington spent two winters near Morristown, partially to guard the foundry. He needed the cannon, muskets, and shot made there to continue to arm the Continental Army. During the civil war and wars subsequent to it, the family foundry made other armaments to supply the armed forces. Some of the earliest automobile parts of Ford's Model A were custom designed and produced in the foundry. MacSimmons Foundry, Inc. continued to supply Ford with parts until the Ford Plant in Mahwah, New Jersey, finally shut its doors in 1983.

By 1991 Brian had his own family, a stay at home wife and three children, and was living comfortably in Sussex Falls, New Jersey. Along with his brothers, Tommy and Pat, he was vice president of the MacSimmons Company. Demand for industrial foundry parts had declined with the American automotive industry. But the boys had a plan. As they took over management of the company from Brian's father and uncle (their uncle only had one child with no interest in the company), they began to branch out the product line. While they still served some of its old manufacturing customers, the majority of their production and sales were in the area of parts for historic recreation (the movie industry especially needed them when they required props) and custom-made auto parts for classic automobiles. The three brothers, all of whom were good friends, were optimistic that they, their seventy workers (many of whom were also part of generations of family who had been employed at the MacSimmons Foundry) and their children would be able to continue the legacy of the business into its 300th year of operation.

Brian and his brothers assumed that they would purchase the company much in the same way previous generations of the MacSimmons family had done so. They would buy the stock on a "purchase money" basis using the stock as underlying collateral to support a promissory note over twenty years to Brian's father and uncle. The company's accountant would supply them with an independent appraisal of the value of the business and the older MacSimmons would receive installment payments amortized over 240 payments at an interest equal to the equivalent treasury bond rate plus 100 basis points (1% above the bond). This is the way it had been done since the business was incorporated in the first decade of the 20th century. The boys were comfortable that the revenue of the business could support these payments. The business was valued at $6,000,000. Brian and his brothers met with the company's attorney to review the papers for the transfer of ownership. Brian's dad was now 62 and recently remarried to a woman in her early 40s. Their mother had passed away five years prior. Uncle Stanton was 60 and since the boys took control of the business he spent most of his days at his Florida home. Brian eagerly looked forward to the meeting with his dad and uncle to complete the transaction. It was his turn now to continue the long tradition of the MacSimmons family and he wondered what people 100 years from now would think when they saw his portrait in the halls of the company's manor house, which was used as a corporate office, along with his many ancestors whose portraits were now so proudly displayed.

At the meeting, dad and uncle had a peculiar look on their face. Brian, sensing that something was wrong, asked his older relations about the nature of the problem. "Sons, I don't know how to tell you this. But your uncle and I have decided to sell the corporation along with all of its assets to a syndicate of attorneys who are going to develop the property. They are going to use our

37 acres here to build high priced condos and keep the manor house as a clubhouse. They are also going to level the foundry building and fire all of our employees. By the way, they offered us $17,000,000 and I am going to move to Florida to be near your uncle with your new step-mom. Sorry about this sons. I wish all of you the best of luck. I know the future now looks hard. But I know my boys, you will recover."

After 290 years of continuous operation through wars, panics, and depressions, MacSimmons Foundry had ceased operation. Brian was now unemployed.

Challenge Questions:

1. Explain how the attorney-developers were able to use a LBO to finance their purchase of the business. Further, how would they make money on this deal?

2. Would you accept $17,000,000 in cash now rather than $6,000,000 plus interest in scheduled payments over 20 years (about $50,186 per month) and in the process terminate the existence of the oldest business in America? (The Moral Issue).

Case 4F
The Case of Crazy Eddie
Was he Insane?

He grew up in a tough section of Flatbush, NY. He was not a good student and he did not attend college. Although he wasn't a big person, he was constantly in fights and wore his wounds from them like a badge of honor. Even as a teenager he was making deals in back alleys. His father owned an electronics business. Later in life the family found success operating a windows display business. With the income derived from his business activities, Sam Antar sometimes struggled to support his wife and four children before becoming a very successful businessman. Eddie did now grow up with a silver spoon in his mouth. But Eddie had a dream.

In the early 1970s, after a string of business setbacks, his father came to the rescue with the financial backing he needed to incorporate his electronics store and get it on a sound footing. His brother, Allen, joined him in the business. Other family members were also given a piece of the business. Eddie's idea was to expand beyond anyone's imagination. His dream was to branch into the fast growing electronics area and become the biggest appliance and electronics merchant around. But the business had limited capital. How would he do it?

With the help of a "creative accountant" Eddie prepared financial statements, which bore no relationship to reality. He made up imaginary assets and cash accounts. He grossly inflated revenues. But the commercial banks did not question the fraudulent financial statements. They provided Crazy Eddie Corporation with a substantial line of credit. With it, Eddie went to the large appliance and electronic manufacturers and was able to

obtain a larger amount in trade credits. He was on his way.

With the help of an Irish actor named Jerry Carroll, pretending to be Eddie, Eddie bought a ton of TV advertising to get his message across. Carroll, the pitchman, would state in the ads "Crazy Eddie, his prices are insane!" Indeed his prices were lower than anyone else. But what did it matter? As long as he pretended to show a profit, the creditors continued to lend and Eddie and his family kept skimming large sums of revenue off the top line of the income statement and adding to their personal fortunes. When the creditors began to balk, Eddie took the company public in 1984 and at $8 a share raised the money he needed to stabilize the business in a public stock offering (the stock would eventually rise to a split-adjusted price of $75). Again the accountants were complicit to certifying the phony financial statements. The public offering permitted Eddie and his family to stabilize the cash position of the company for a while and to skim even more from the top. At one point the corporation operated forty-three large retail warehouses and stores in four states.

During all this time, Eddie became a celebrity on his own right. With his stash of cash, he hung out with scores of well-known models and actresses. He was a regular at the best and most exclusive clubs in New York. He owned a fleet of cars and vacation homes. He went to parties and traveled the world with the most beautiful people. For almost 20 years, Eddie was living a dream.

However, by 1993, the cash from the public offering was running out. The low price structure was not producing enough revenue to replenish inventory, pay overhead and continue to feed tons of cash to Eddie and the family. Creditors, investors and the SEC began to ask questions. Even Eddie's own independent auditors woke up (belated of course) from their lethargy and began to probe the books with renewed interest. Eddie had run out of luck. After four years of SEC probes, civil suits and criminal investigations, Eddie and the family were brought down and their personal assets seized. In 1997, a federal judge sentenced Eddie to eight years in a federal prison. From his perch on high, Eddie ended up slinging hash in a prison kitchen. He was released for good behavior after less than two years in prison and became a free man on parole.

His nephew, Sam Antar (Allen's son), opened an electronic store in Wayne, New Jersey. Building on his Uncle's reputation the store was called "Crazy Eddie's". Eddie and Allen became paid consultants to Sam's business.

Challenge Questions:

1. Explain the legal mechanisms by which investors and creditors were able to obtain access to the personal assets of Crazy Eddie and his family?

2. Until 1993, Crazy Eddie lived the life style of a multi-millionaire and celebrity. Four years later in 1997, he was in prison because of his fraud. Would you do it? (The Moral Issue).

Case 4G
Brenna's Fun World -Revisited

Brenna Donigan had a dream. As she looked at the abandoned ruin of the once famous Big Daddy's Palace on the Blue Stream Highway in Staten Island, she saw a way by which she could support her family and help her community. The BD Palace had closed its doors for good, three years ago, after a gruesome daylight homicide and hit on the founder and owner of the large adult club "Big Daddy" Duke Smith. Whether it was a mob hit, as many people claimed, or an act of revenge by Lexi May, one of his former girlfriends, and her friend, Tara Bianco, the police never did find the answer. The only evidence the police had was that two brunette haired and slender women shrouded with hoods over their heads came into the "Palace" with a machine gun and sprayed the club and its owner, Big Daddy, with bullets. Since that event, the busy club had closed and stayed that way for years.

With the money she received from an employee buyout from the management consulting firm for whom she formerly worked, Brenna had purchased the building and intended to create a business entity to own and operate a family centered "Fun World". Along with two friends from college, Torrey and Cat, she hoped their business would be able to create a family-friendly experience, a place much different than the sordid adult club of the Big Daddy days. Her dream was to turn the 18,000 square foot facility into a place where families could dine together on traditional fare while their children participated, before and after dinner, in games and rides where a child's imagination could be set free. Brenna's Fun World would be a combination of a traditional diner and amusement park in one.

Brenna was convinced that her business would be successful and would be the start of a turnaround of businesses in her community from the seedy legacy of the Big Daddy era.

Challenge Questions:

1. Explain how the process of promotion, incorporation and organization of the corporation would apply to the ideas of Brenna, Torrey and Cat. In other words, how would they go about creating this business?

2. If your community had fallen into social disrepair caused by spurious businesses like Big Daddy's Palace, would you be willing to start a new business venture to alter the social fabric of the area? (The Moral Issue).

Case 4H
The Unsigned Resignation Letter

Since he was 24 years old, Direct Tools, Inc. (DTI) had employed Alex Brusca. At 46 years old, he was appointed President and CEO of the company. DTI was sold to a large fortune 500 company six years later, but Alex remained the President of the Corporation, which was now organized in a parent-subsidiary arrangement as one of the four divisions of Connecticut Industrial Holdings Corporation (CIHC), a publicly held corporation. For the next five years, Alex maintained a profitable operation at the union based division, no small feat in a time of rapid changes in the competitive international marketplace for machine tools and dyes.

Although he was President of DTI, Alex reported to the Vice President of Operations for CIHC, Sam Waters. Sam was in charge of operations for all four divisions. Sam was ten years younger than Alex and possessed an MBA degree from Harvard Business School. Alex had a BA in accounting from a local New Jersey college. Sam believed that all of CIHC divisions should be managed by younger officers with MBA educations from elite institutions and often sparred with Alex over the ways and means by which DTI met its targets. While DTI did meet the goals set by corporate, Alex resented the fact that his division was compelled to achieve "cash cow" goals far in excess of the those set for other divisions.

Matters came to a head at a corporate retreat when Alex explained that if corporate HQ wished for him to achieve new goals set for his division, then corporate had to relieve him of the time he was expending on audit, control and assessment reports. Alex wanted to spend more time dealing with production, labor and sales problems. To Alex, that was the key to success; working with employees and customers in New Jersey where the division was located, rather than having meetings and finishing reports to the corporate offices in Fairfield, Connecticut. The way Sam saw it a clean sweep was necessary.

One brisk late March day, Sam drove down to the West Caldwell, New Jersey, facility of DTI and unexpectedly demanded a meeting with Alex who had just arrived back to the office from a breakfast meetings with a new customer. Sam told Alex that the old ways had to change and that CICH needed "younger managers" with better academic training. Sam had prepared a resignation letter for Alex to sign. He would leave it on his desk and expected him to sign it and clean out his office by the end of the business day. If he signed the letter, Alex would be given six months of severance pay. At 57 years CIHC security personnel locked old Alex out of his office as president of the company. All he had to show for his 33 years of work was two boxes of personal affects brought out to his car.

As he sat in his car on his way back to his home, Alex made a decision. He wouldn't sign the letter. Instead, he would call an attorney to review his options. A young attorney, James Parnell, was assigned to his case.

Challenge Questions:

1. Under the New Jersey Corporations Law (NJ follows the RMBCA), was Alex terminated in a lawful way?

2. What causes of actions does Alex possess to challenge Sam's decision to terminate him?

3. Do you believe that CIHC has a right as an organization to sweep out older managers in order to change its ways? (The Moral Issue).

Case Exercise 4I
Is This a Good Investment?

The Olympic Motel was sold for $10,000,000 to the "Doctors Investment Group, LP" a limited partnership consisting of the following individuals as limited partners:

Dr. Melissa Deeb, an internal medicine specialist

Dr. Kelsey Spangs, a cardiologist

Dr. Landers Engleman, a pediatrician and

Dr. Moe Middleton, a proctologist

Each doctor put up the sum of $250,000 for one of the four limited partnership units. Prior to the purchase all of the physicians had successful practices and each was taxed at the 36% marginal tax rate on their adjusted income. A mortgage note of $9,000,000 secured by the motel was obtained to complete the necessary financing. The allocation for the purchase was as follows:

$7,000,000 to Buildings and Improvements

$2,400,000 to Furniture and Fixtures

$ 600,000 to Land

During the first year of ownership the Motel experienced these results:

$2,000,000 in Operating Revenue

$1,600,000 in Operating Expenses

$(550,000) in Interest Expenses

Hence the LP had:

$(150,000) Net Operating Revenue

$(254,000) Depreciation on Buildings and Improvements (SL Method)

$(480,000) Depreciation on Furniture and Fixtures (DDB Method)

$(884,000) Total Income (Loss)

Challenge Questions:

1. Do you think that physician group made a good
    investment in this case?

2. Do you think that the federal tax code is fair? If you
    were a highly compensated individual would you take
    advantage of it? (The Moral Issue).

CHAPTER 5
SECURITIES LAW

Case 5A
Beagle Computer

Three college students started Beagle Computer in 1982 while they were juniors at the University of Pennsylvania. The students were Steve Frolic, and two of his boyhood friends, Hahn Justinus and Bennet Justinus, fraternal twins. Steve, Hahn, and Ben were all originally from the Philadelphia area. In college, Steve was an accounting and mathematics major. Hahn was a finance/information system major and Ben was a major in computer engineering. Building on a design Ben had developed for a project in college, the boys developed a prototype for a mini computer, which could accomplish the tasks of most of the mainframes of their day but at a much lower cost. Further, the new design would only use 1/50 of the space of the normal mainframe.

With the patent for their design at hand, the boys headed to Silicon Valley in California right after college to connect with the computer and systems people who could help them with their goal of improving their prototype and turning it into a commercially feasible project. They promoted, incorporated and organized Beagle Computer, Inc., a Delaware corporation doing business in California. A venture capital firm, Hunter Capital, LLC, provided $500,000 in venture financing to the boys. In return Hunter took back a 40% interest in the equity of the corporation. After two years, in 1985, Beagle went to market with its first computer and it became an instant success. Businesses especially could not get enough of the Beagles and it was clear that the clumsy mainframes from HP and IBM left much to be desired as compared to the roll in mini computer from Beagle. Wang Labs and Prime Computer produced similar products but Beagle's operating system proved to be faster and more powerful and their models were slightly less expensive. To obtain the capital they needed to build an office building and manufacturing facility and to get the cash to mass produce and market their computers, Hunter Capital brought in Silverman Godscholl in 1988 to take the company public. Silverman suggested that the company issue 20,000,000 shares at $10 a share.

The owners of the privately held corporation were Steve (20% of the stock), Hahn (20% of the stock), Ben (20% of the stock) and Hunter Capital (40% of the stock). When the company was incorporated it included a special provision in its articles of incorporation, which permitted the exercise of preemptive subscription rights. The preemptive rights provision allowed each shareholder to subscribe to a number of shares in any stock offering at the initial offering price in order to allow the shareholder with the rights to maintain their proportional ownership of the corporation. On the morning of the day on which Silverman brought out the IPO, Steve exercised his preemptive right to purchase 4,000,000 shares of the company. He needed $40,000,000 to do so, but he was able to get his financing he needed from a consortium of commercial and investment banks. Steve's decision brought immediate results. By 2 pm on the first day of trading the stock went from the IPO price of $10 a share to $38. Steve called his broker and requested that the broker sell 1,500,000 shares at minimum ask price of $34 a share. Volume was heavy and the broker was able to sell the shares at an average price of $35. It seemed that everyone wanted some Beagle shares. With the $51,000,000 from the sale, Steve was able to pay back his loans and had over $10,500,000 in cash to play with as well as stock worth $85,000,000. It had been a good day in Steve's life and the 28 year old saw a bright future ahead. Little did he know?

Three weeks prior to the IPO Steve had married Meredith Dorno. Meredith graduated form Boise State University in Idaho in 1986 with a double major in Sociology and Education. Although an excellent student, Meredith was unable to find a teaching position in Idaho and headed to California with some of her sorority sisters from college. They settled in the Bay area but

Meredith was only able to obtain employment at Mendes' Fruit Juice Bar and Grill. The job was tough on Meredith but she did like the clientele, many of whom worked in the Silicon Valley. One group of guys from Pennsylvania in particular seemed pleasant and was great tippers. The group consisted of Steve, Hahn and Ben. Steve was especially fond of Meredith and after a period of flirtation and hesitation, Meredith agreed to go out with Steve. Dating turned into love and love became marriage. Since Steve's fortunes seemed so bright and California was a community property state, Steve's attorney demanded that they execute a pre-marital agreement. Meredith consented to Steve's request but insisted that Steve also execute a Will designating her as the heir of his residuary estate. Steve, deeply in love, agreed.

At 4 PM on the day of the IPO, Steve was elated. All of his dreams had come true. He had $10,500,00 in cash in the bank, $85,000,000 in stock and the thought of more to come. Steve decided to treat himself. He drove his car to the Bay Area Maserati dealership and purchased the most expensive car on the lot. In his excitement he drove the new car to his home in Palo Alto to show off to Meredith and to tell her the good news about the IPO. Unfamiliar with the car and driving at an excessive speed on the serpentine and hilly roads of the Bay Area, Steve lost control of the vehicle, ran through an inadequate metal barrier and plummeted to his death in a rocky canyon below. Experts estimate that Steve was still alive and had conscious thoughts for at least three minutes before his car exploded in sight of the beautiful Pacific Ocean.

Challenge Questions:

1. How do we obtain Preemptive Subscription Rights?

2. Why are they so valuable?

3. Why do so few people exercise them?

4. If you were Meredith, (at age 24 and worth $100,000,000 or so) would you ever be able to get over the tragedy of Steve's death? (The Moral Issue).

Case 5B
Meeting the Devil?

It took a while for college students James Parnell, Ken Kravitz, and Gary Benes to scrape together the $52 that they needed for one Chase Bancorp share of stock. They also had to pay a $25 commission to a stockbroker to place the trade. But then the day came; Parnell, Kravitz, and Benes were concurrent owners together of one share of stock. The odd thing was that they did not buy the stock as an investment. The three friends had another purpose in mind.

As expected, about two months after receiving their one share, the boys were invited to attend and participate in the annual shareholders' meeting of the Chase Manhattan Bank Corporation. The college students were eagerly looking forward to this chance. On the day of the 10 am meeting, the boys awoke at 5 am and drove 140 miles up the turnpike from Philadelphia to New York City. Arriving in New York, the friends had breakfast together. His first time in the city, Gary commented how expensive everything was. By 9:30 am the college friends had arrived at Rockefeller Center and took the escalator up to the third floor auditorium where the annual meeting of the Chase Bank Holdings Corporation was about to be held.

Finally, he was there. David Rockefeller himself. To the boys Rockefeller was the epitome of all the capitalist evil in the world. The friends were among those who believed that a small group of Capitalists would meet from time to time with a select group from the Soviet Politburo to determine and control world affairs. Such a view of the world was not uncommon on college campuses in the 1970s. To the boys' surprise, David Rockefeller was a pleasant looking man with a genial manner and style. After a brief presentation on Chase's financial results, Rockefeller (as CEO of Chase) asked the small group of gathered shareholders if they had any questions. The boys were ready to do what they came to do.

Ken had the first question. "Isn't it true Mr. Rockefeller that you have a partnership with Monsanto Corporation and together you finance the production of chemical munitions which are used to burn babies in Southeast Asia?" Rockefeller, calmly and without a trace of anger in his voice replied, "Monsanto does have a deposit account at our bank. However, we neither lend money to them nor do we finance any of their production activities. We do not and would not ever condone a company which produced anything that could be used to harm children." It was now Parnell's turn: "Mr. Rockefeller isn't it true that you and other wealthy capitalists have regular meetings with members of the Soviet Politburo where you plan and control world affairs for your own evil purposes?" Parnell was proud of himself; this time the miserable capitalist was not going to be able to hide his nefarious activities. Rockefeller politely replied with a slight smile: "the only member of the Soviet Politburo that I have ever met was Andrei Gromyko at a UN fund raiser. We shook hands when we were introduced and talked a little about the weather. That was the beginning and end of our conversation." Gary had an equally pointed question, which Rockefeller answered with the same grace and patience. As the meeting ended, Rockefeller left the podium, came down into the auditorium seats and approached the boys. "Boys, if you have any other questions or wish to just chat with me, feel free to do so. If you don't want to talk here, we can go up to the penthouse. I am sure I could arrange to have some lunch sent up to us." The boys thanked Rockefeller but declined the invitation.

Shaken, Parnell thought to himself as he was driving west out of NYC, that maybe he was wrong about David Rockefeller. After all, Rockefeller proved to be a pretty nice guy. And if he was wrong about Rockefeller, perhaps his whole view about the evils of capitalism had to be reconsidered. He had much to think about.

Challenge Questions:

1. Why was Chase Manhattan Corporation obligated to have an annual meeting? Further, why did the boys have the right to attend the meeting?

2. Do you think the college students in this challenge case acted in a rude manner? What is your own view about large publicly traded corporation? Do they exert too much influence on world affairs? (The Moral Issue).

Case 5C
Burpee Feed and Seed

Burpee Feed and Seed is a world leader in direct sales of consumer landscaping products. Through online sales and direct marketing by members of non-profit organizations, Burpee created a business model, which generated substantial sales and profits without the need for "brick and mortar" stores. Burpee also had a reputation for quality products at a reasonable price – a combination that has increased its share in its market.

Karl Linden, a famous takeover artist, saw potential in the Burpee franchise. Linden believed that if his LBO group purchased the corporation, he could leverage its well-accepted brands to include other consumer products, thereby increasing sales of the direct marketer by several fold. Burpee's share price has always been a solid performer but being a consumer-based company its returns never far outdistanced the general stock market.

James Parnell, an investor in Burpee, read in the financial press that Linden might have an interest in Burpee. Doing his own due diligence as an investor, Parnell thought that if Linden purchased the corporation that he would have to offer much more than the $22 a share – the price at which the stock was selling in the present market. But it seemed like new information about Burpee was no longer being circulated in the media. What was happening?

Parnell, aware of his right to inspect the books, records and stock lists of the company, called Burpee's headquarters in California. Eventually his call was routed to an officer in investor relations. The Assistant Director of Investor Relations, Sheryl Majors, spoke with him. Parnell began his questioning. "Was Linden making an offer for the company"? Majors declined to answer. "Had Linden met with the Board"? Again there was no response. "Would it be ok if Parnell flew to California to visit the corporate headquarters and reviewed the company's records as was his rights under the law?" Majors needed to end the conversation. She stated "Sir, Mr. Linden is meeting right now with the Board – I cannot answer any more questions."

Parnell was satisfied. He entered an order to double his stock holdings. His purchase price was $22. Two days later Burpee announced that it was being acquired by Linden for $40 a share.

Challenge Questions:

1. In your opinion, did Parnell make a good investment?

2. How did Parnell's rights under the RMBCA assist him in making a decision?

3. Do you believe that it is fair of some investors to use legal information to make financial decisions, even if other investors lose money? (The Moral Issue).

Case 5D
The Shane Madison Company

The Shane Madison Company (SMC) is a privately held corporation started by well-known accountant and investor, Shane Madison. The company is in essence a holding company that opportunistically purchases majority positions in small but growing companies that manufacture goods or provide services that take advantage of foreign currency fluctuations, thus recapturing market share from international competitors. Shane did not come up with this business concept - rather it was expostulated by one of her college professors, the legendary James Parnell. With the help of a small business development grant she developed the concept into a formidable business strategy that has netted her (and the other handful of shareholders in her company) extraordinary profits.

After a series of failed marriages, one of the SMC's investors, Lon Desmond, needs to sell his shares. Shane is concerned that Lon may sell his shares to her chief business nemesis, Garland Smith. Smith, stealing her ideas, has managed to gain some traction in out-bidding Shane for some valuable business assets and companies. Shane is concerned that if Garland gets his hands on Lon's shares or any of the other investors' equity interests, life will become difficult for her and Garland may emerge as the leader in this lucrative activity. The thought of Shane being over-taken by Garland seems fundamentally unfair to Shane and she cannot live with this possibility.

Shane has hired you to come up with some proposals on how stop Garland from making this transfer. For now, Lon is just thinking about transferring his shares; he has not elicited private bids for them.

Challenge Questions:

1. Does the RMBCA permit restrictions on a shareholders' transfer of stock?

2. What suggestions or options exist to restrict the transfer of an investor's share? Further, what requirements does the law impose before restrictions can be considered enforceable?

3. Do you believe that it is fair for Shane to take advantage of Lon by coming up with ways to restrict his transfer if it is results in Lon receiving reduced consideration for the sale of his shares? (The Moral Issue).

Case 5E
The International Horse Case

She started with just a few horses. But soon word spread that Jelly Kones bred the best horses in the world. Indeed, the rich and famous from all over the world came to the Circle JK ranch in Glen Argyll, Pennsylvania, to see the many fine animals raised by Jelly and her associates. The JK brand was known for purity and superior quality. Why not use the brand to license merchandise and start a worldwide franchise operation? Jelly saw the potential to make hundreds of millions.

With her ideas roughly scratched out on three simple sheets of paper, Jelly made an appointment to visit A. Erik Sullivan, the CEO of the internationally famous venture capital boutique, Omega Capital, Inc. After a thorough analysis by his chief accountant, Omega has estimated that JK Enterprises would need at least $12,000,000 in start-up capital.   They also estimate that on a conservative basis, the new JK operation could easily make $4,000,000 a year during the first five years of its operation.

Omega also suggests that Jelly take her business international. The firm believes that the rising prosperity of Asia and the petro-monarchies of the Middle East might be the place to start. Erik and Jelly fly off to the Kingdom of the Kutar Emirates, an oil rich and horse-crazy country. Their twin goals are to obtain the capital they need for expansion and to open their first franchise operation in the Emirate and use that operation as a template for other foreign ventures. The Sheik of Kutar, his Royal Highness Khalad Aharri, is a difficult person with whom to get an audience. His Prime Minister, Premier Ahmed Johno, has offered to assist the group in obtaining a meeting with the Shiek, but he demands a substantial gift of cash to arrange for the conference.

Jelly asks Omega for advice.   Much is at stake.

Challenge Questions:

1. In your opinion does the "Foreign Corrupt Practices Act" apply to this transaction?

2. Assuming that Jelly's return is about half of the projected profits over the next five years, do you think that she is morally obligated to share her new found wealth with charitable causes that benefit both animals and humankind? Further would you urge her to accept Premier Ahmed Johno's terms for an audience? (The Moral Issue).

Case 5F
Colorado Mattress Co., Inc.

As the four men walked across the 7th hole of the golf course, Harold became nostalgic. It seemed amazing to him that all of them had been friends since they had memories. When they were little boys they had first met at their common place of worship each weekend. All had gone to college in Kentucky and had shared college experiences. And now here they were, in their early sixties - still buddies playing golf on Friday mornings as they had done each week for the last 30 years.

Now pillars of the community, the four had lived peaceful and prosperous lives in Knoxville, Tennessee. Harold Goldman owned a chain of successful jewelry stores; Keith Palkin was a respected orthodontist; Stanley Levin operated and owned six local Dairy King franchises and Monty Kalpers was a former manager and majority partner in closely held NK Mining and Minerals, Inc. All of the men were members of community and philanthropic organizations in the Greater Knoxville areas and at one time, each had been on the board of directors of the local Kiwanis Society. Further, all were married and lived in the upscale River Heights area right outside the city limits.

As the men approached the tee for the 8th hole, Monty could hear Keith and Harold laughing about something. Stan had noticed the same thing. It was not like these good friends to fail to share a joke among them. When confronted, at first Keith and Harold would not respond to Monty's request for an explanation about what it was that the two men found to be so funny. After some harassing, Keith finally broke the news.

Harold's son, Trevor, was a vice-president of Colorado

Mattress Co., Inc. The company was one of the three largest mattress producers in North America. Its brands were known far and wide but in recent years the company was struggling to make a profit due to increasing foreign competition, a bloated management structure and labor costs which had gotten out of control in its union organized manufacturing plants. Doyle Capital, a well-known venture capital firm had approached management about a leverage buyout of CMC. Rumors had circulated and the stock price had recently moved from $11 a share to $15. On Sunday of the previous week, Trevor had spoke to his father and expressed his concern about his future. Harold asked Trevor why he was worried. After some probing, Trevor finally admitted that Doyle Capital and CMC had entered into a secret agreement for Doyle to purchase CMC for $24 a share and that the takeover of CMC should be completed in about two months at which time it was likely that Trevor would be out of work. How was he going to support himself, his wife Kiera (and their two daughters, Carly and Katie) when that happened? Trevor was most distressed about the future.

Harold was sad at the news about his son's imminent unemployment. However, at $12 a share he also saw an opportunity for a good investment. He called up his stockbroker, Vince Melosi, at Stinson Gehman and ordered the initial purchase of 2,000 shares. As the price climbed Harold bought an additional 7,000 shares and was attempting to access a line of credit through his business to triple that amount of stock. On Wednesday of that week, Harold and Keith had dinner and Harold's wife broke the news about possible changes at CMC and her concern for her son. Seeing an opportunity, Keith, who also traded through an account managed by Vince Melosi, bought a block of 10,000 shares of CMC on Thursday at $13 a share. By Friday morning before their golf date, the shares were already up to $15 and that was the reason why the two men (Harold and Keith) were giddy with laughter about their good investment.

Harold and Keith finally went clean with their pals, Stan and Monty. Without finishing the game, Stan and Monty immediately went to the clubhouse and in a private area called Vince Melosi. Each purchased sizable blocks of CMC and the price went up again that day. Vince did not know what was going on for sure, but he knew his four clients to be cautious businessmen. Usually they purchased shares in small quantities. Purchasing 10,000 share blocks was highly unusual. Vince could smell something cooking. On Monday of the following week he called his "A" list customers and told them to put everything they could spare into CMC. Vince also bought 30,000 shares for his own account.

Two weeks after that Monday, Doyle Capital announced their takeover of the venerable company at $24 a share. All of the men in Knoxville (subsequently called the "Knoxville 4"), Vince the broker and his customers had made considerable sums of money. For the first few weeks the men counted their good fortunes. Collectively they had made millions in capital gains and trading profits in the CMC trade. It was a happy time for them.

Less than two months after the takeover on a sultry business day in June, Vince received a phone call from Stock Watch, an investigation unit of the federal SEC. Investigators had noticed unusual trading activity out of the Knoxville office of Stinson Gehman. A team from the SEC was coming out to review and take the records from the local office. Stinson had promised that they would fully cooperate with the government investigation and if any wrongdoing were found, they would take appropriate action.

Challenge Questions:

1. In your opinion was there any liability under the 1934 Securities and Exchange and/or SEC Rule 10b-5 for the trading activities of Harold in this case?

2. In your opinion are Monty, Stan and Keith also potentially liable?

3. Vince had no direct knowledge of the takeover, is he potentially liable under SEC Rule 10b-5?

4. Trevor, now unemployed, did not trade or make a penny on the deal. Should he be held liable for any violations of the law?

5. If you knew for sure that a company was being taken over at price, which would produce a gain of 125% in a few weeks, would you act on such information? (The Moral Issue).

Case 5G
Creating a Monster in MGT 327

Albert Coffey was a quiet student. He sat in the back row of the classroom in Comstock Hall and rarely participated in class discussions. Dr. Parnell had a difficult time remembering his name.

The time came for a discussion of securities regulation laws, often a dry subject to students in the class. As the discussion turned into exemptions to the requirements of the 1933 Securities Act, Albert's demeanor changed and he seemed to come alive. Albert was particularly interested in SEC Regulation "A". The quiet student virtually monopolized the class discussion with one question after another. After class, Albert followed Parnell to his office and continued to ask questions about the exemption. As a class project, Albert wrote a fifteen-page term paper on Regulation "A". Parnell was very impressed by this work. It was clear that Albert knew more about the regulation than anyone else in Parnell's acquaintance.

Parnell soon forgot about the quiet student as the years passed. Parnell was working for a law firm in Lehigh County, which represented a number of physician groups and practices. A specialist in corporate and business law, the senior partners of the firm asked Parnell to review a request from one of its physician clients. The client had received a letter from a promoter of a real estate venture asking if they had any interest (for the sum of $150,000 per unit) in buying a part of a limited partnership, which had purchased a commercial office building in Emmaus, PA. Parnell perused the letter for its legality. It also seemed to him that the success of the venture depended on future prospects for the commercial property market. While market prices have been increasing in value by about 12% per annum, over the last five years, there was no certainty that past gains would produce future ones. Parnell advised the client not to purchase any units.

Parnell was, however, impressed by the content of the three-page letter. It was clearly legally correct in both form and substance. The writer of the letter knew what he was doing. The offering was taking advantage of Regulation "A" in raising capital to finance the project. One thing that troubled Parnell was the "rip" (the amount taken by the promoter as compensation for packaging the deal). It was 15% of the total. The total value of the deal was $1,800,000. At that level of pricing, the Promoter would receive $240,000. Not a bad deal for about six months of work and very little risk to him.

Then Parnell had the shock of his life. The promoter and issuer of the letter was none other than Albert Coffey! Parnell instantly picked up the phone. Was it the same Albert who was in his class at Monrovia? The secretary in his office put Parnell on hold - then a familiar voice came on the line. It was Albert. Promoting real estate deals through Regulation "A" offerings was what Albert was doing since he left college. According to Albert this was his 14th deal. Albert made a lot of money since leaving college. Soon thereafter, the commercial property market collapsed.

Challenge Questions:

1. Explain how promoters of these "Regulation A" deals make money on commercial real estate projects?

2. What are the risks of such deals for the potential class of equity investors?

3. Do you think that 15% to 20% of the total project costs are justified as a commission in these deals?

4. Would you consider being a promoter of such deals or do you believe that it is morally wrong to take advantage of investors by shifting the risk of such deals to them and taking such large commissions? (The Moral Issue).

Case 5H
Lindsay's Legacy

Lindsay Daniels was a very successful businesswoman. Through hard work and effort, she managed to become the first woman CEO of Mega-Bucks, Inc., a fortune 500 company. Her personal life, however, was not as happy. After five failed marriages and a TV appearance on the reality show "Survivor", Lindsay stopped any additional attempts at matrimony. At 38 years old she was at the top of the business ladder when the unthinkable happened. While sailing on her 72-foot yacht in the Atlantic Ocean toward Bar Harbor, Maine, the perfect storm hit. Her yacht, named "The Jelly Doughnut", was sunk and all aboard, including Lindsay, taken down with her.

Lindsay's estate is valued at $43,000,000. Five months before her demise, she executed a new last will and testament. In it she specifically excluded her many ex husbands and inserted as her residuary legatee, her best friend from College, Brielle Carrere. Brielle, shocked at her friend's death was equally shocked by the large size of the legacy she received.

Now an unwed mother with seven children living in a small log cabin with a plow horse named Buster outside of Nazareth, Pennsylvania, Brielle doesn't know how to invest her great fortune. She has come to you to ask how she should manage her money. The shrewd Brielle has offered you an annual fee of 10% of whatever GAINS you receive on her investments.

Challenge Questions:

1. How would you divide Brielle's portfolio? Further, what factors would you consider before making investments on her behalf?

2. If you were Brielle, would you donate a portion of you newfound wealth to a 501(c) organization like Monrovia College (perhaps in the name of James Parnell – Lindsay's favorite professor) or would you keep all of the money yourself? (The Moral Issue).

CHAPTER 6
BUSINESS TORTS AND INSURANCE

Case 6A
An Invasion of Privacy?

Bill Mathis decided that things needed to change. He had just been appointed general manager of the Lehigh Valley division of ABC Products, Inc., part of a large fortune 500 company. Costs were out of control and he knew that corporate headquarters was thinking of closing the plant unless he could return the plant to profitability. Insurance and workers' compensation claims were off the charts. A reduction in claims to levels in line with national averages would get him half the way there. Bill's first task was to fire the genial human resources manager and replace him with Chuck Savage, a veteran of the 82nd Airborne Division. What Chuck lacked in human resources experience he easily made up with his intensity. After reviewing the records, Chuck was convinced that most of the insurance and workers' compensation claims were phony and bogus. He hired the Ace Detective Agency to investigate all claims and to maintain surveillance of repeated claimants.

One repeated claimant was Wade Caskins. In his five years at ABC, Wade had made six claims for compensation. All were based on back injuries due to heavy lifting. Ultrasound tests and other diagnostic testing did not show any muscle tears or physical injuries. Most of the medical evidence to support Wade's claims came from chiropractors and general practitioners who diagnosed Wade's soft tissue injuries based upon an office examination and patient interview. Chuck called Ace and asked them to place a private investigator on the tail of Wade to see if he was faking.

Wade, a union employee, was dating Anna Soros, a non-union office clerk who also worked at ABC. One day while Wade was on disability leave, Anna took a sick day. Ace sent a young and energetic investigator to conduct surveillance on Wade. The investigator, Slim Leonhard, followed Wade and Anna to Cedar Park in Allentown on a brilliant May Day. Wade and Anna walked to a pine covered area of the park across the stream from Crest Hill College. The area was very secluded. The couple walked into the middle of the pine grove, away from the stares of any other park visitors. Slim followed without being noticed. Slim lay on his stomach on a bed of soft pine needles behind and below a thick flowering bush. He began taking photos of the couple. What he saw seemed to suggest that Wade was able to do things that clearly a person could not do with a back injury. As a matter of fact for the extended time Slim stayed there shooting photos, he was quite impressed with Wade's back strength and endurance and with Anna's dexterity.

Chuck had the evidence the Ace agency provided him. With it Bill and Chuck decided to call in the union president, Andy Kurtz, and the union's attorney, James Parnell. Grinning from ear to ear, the managers confronted Andy and Parnell with an envelope entitled, "Confidential, Do Not Look." They invited Andy and Parnell to review the photos. Parnell was so disgusted with the graphic nature of the photos that he was only able to look at them for an hour or so. But he knew that Wade's workers' compensation case was a non-starter. The union president agreed with Parnell's assessment.

Through some mechanism unknown to them, employees at ABC quickly became aware of the company's actions and it seemed, somehow, many had seen the photographs. Anna was deeply embarrassed to the point where she became physically sick from the incident. Other employees too began to ask the question, do they have photos and a file on me too?

Challenge Questions:

1. Reviewing the elements of the Tort of the Invasion of Privacy, do you believe that Wade Caskins has a good case at law against the company and its investigation firm?

2. Reviewing the elements of the Torts of the Invasion of Privacy and Emotional Distress, do you believe that Anna Soros has a good case at law against the company and its investigation firm?

3. If you were the investigator working on the surveillance of Wade and Anna, would you have sat there and taken pictures of would you have respected their privacy and left the scene? (The Moral Issue).

Case 6B
An Attractive Nuisance

The day was long in coming but finally it was here. Jara Ling had managed to save enough money to put a down payment on a house in a stable neighborhood in Bay Meadows. As a divorced woman, Jara was completely on her own. Buying a house alone was quite an accomplishment and today, closing day, all of the sacrifices, savings and extra hours at work seemed worth it.

Jara was looking at her backyard. It needed work. Grass seed had to be planted and new shrubs and mulch added. There was also a rusted out swing set, which had clearly seen better days. When Spring came, Jara thought she would scrape off the rust, get new chains and paint it bright orange. Her two nephews, Min and Han, might want to visit more often, if there was a swing set out back. Besides, Jara herself might want to be a mother someday, why take it down?

The neighbors next door, the Andersons, also seemed like nice people. Their precocious six year old daughter, Mantha, seemed like a lively girl. Mantha often would stop by to say hello and babble on to Jara. Then it happened.

Jara was at work and returned at the end of long, tiring early spring day. To her horror, she saw Mantha in the backyard. Little Mantha was unconscious. Later, Jara found out that little Mantha had come over to Jara's backyard after school and was swinging on her rusted out swing set when the set fell apart and a rusty bar had hit Mantha on the head. Mantha was rushed to the hospital. She survived but the doctors do not know what affect the accident will have on her long-term health. Mantha's brain function is impair

Challenge Questions:

1. Assuming extensive injuries to Mantha, what legal theory in tort law could be used as a basis for a lawsuit against Jara?

2. In your opinion is Jara liable to Mantha and her parents as her guardians for Mantha's injuries?

3. If you were Mantha's parents, would you forego the right to sue a neighbor with whom you previously had good relations or would you bring a suit against Jara? (The Moral Issue).

Case 6C
The Punch

Leslie Gasper was having a tough day. As the newly appointed Vice President of Operations, it was her job to reduce employment at HDS Financial (A Division of NW Mega bank) by 25%. Pink slips were sent out that day to the laid off workers and Leslie could feel the anger from the glares of the fired employees as they were escorted from the building. Leslie felt frustrated because she was just carrying out her instructions. Didn't they realize she was just doing her job?

Leslie's boss, Martin Evans, was also feeling the heat. Martin was asked to work a miracle at HDS. A native of Wisconsin, Martin still felt like a stranger in the Lehigh Valley; but he knew he was making progress and believed that corporate HQ in Chicago would eventually recognize his success in making HDS profitable. The one person that always seemed to understand him at work was Leslie. Leslie was bright, attractive and an easy person with whom to communicate. Martin had no regrets about promoting her to VP of Operations over more senior managers, even though she was only 34 years old.

Leslie had recently divorced. She had no children. Her divorce was an amicable one. She and her husband had just grown apart. Sometimes she missed being married and had started on occasion to see her ex-husband again - just as friends. Martin and his wife, Gretchen, had settled in Nazareth, Pennsylvania with their three children. At first Gretchen felt lonely in Pennsylvania, but her neighbors were friendly and she had become part of a network of stay-at-home moms. She also was beginning to feel at home in her spacious and comfortable suburban house. Then it happened.

Martin worked long hours but usually called home first and let Gretchen know if he wouldn't be there for dinner. That Thursday night, Gretchen decided to make Martin's favorite dish and was excited at the prospect of dinner that night. By 6:30 pm all was ready, but Martin did not appear. At 7 pm, Gretchen called HDS, but was told that Martin had left a few minutes before. By 8 pm, Martin still had not returned home. Gretchen was worried.

The stress of that workday was hard on Leslie. While talking to Martin about it, Leslie did the one thing she swore she would never do; she began to cry. Martin, feeling sorry for Leslie's plight asked her to go out for a drink with him at Fruit Juice Works, an upscale bar in historic downtown Bethlehem. Leslie was happy to go.

By 9 o'clock, Gretchen was losing it. Martin was not home, not at work and had not called her. She called Mary Schaffer, Martin's secretary, at Mary's home. Mary told Gretchen that Martin had left at about 6:30 pm with Leslie Gasper and that she thought she overheard them saying that they were going to a place in downtown Bethlehem. At 10 o'clock, Gretchen asked her 14-year-old daughter to watch the other children and left her suburban house and headed to Bethlehem. By 11:15 pm, after driving for a while and visiting three other bars in Bethlehem, Gretchen walked into the Fruit Juice Works Bar. The bar area was mostly free of customers. There was a bartender cleaning glasses with his back behind the two remaining customers. The customers were Martin and Leslie. Gretchen could see the couple close to each other; indeed Martin's hand was resting on Leslie's thigh. They were looking into each other's eyes.

Gretchen overcome with emotion and anger walked up to Leslie. According to Leslie's account (without any words or provocation) Gretchen with all her might punched Leslie in the face. Leslie fell off the barstool and temporarily lost consciousness. Martin helped her up with the bartender's help.

She did not seek medical attention. Gretchen claimed that the two women had pushed and shoved each other and in the process of a fair fight she hit Leslie. *Things happened so fast that the bartender only saw Leslie on the ground and nothing beforehand. Only Martin had witnessed the entire incident.*

Upon reflection, Leslie was mad. She had not had an affair with Martin and she felt victimized by Gretchen's attack. As a private affiant she pressed criminal charges for assault 3 (Simple Assault) a misdemeanor of the 1st degree, a serious crime. She asked a skilled attorney, James Parnell, to advise her on the case and to appear in court as her counsel. Parnell agreed to do so. On the date of trial, to Parnell's surprise, reporters from the local TV stations and newspapers were present inside and outside the courtroom. A female judge was assigned to hear the case. Parnell knew that the case depended on Martin's testimony. A very competent female attorney represented Gretchen. Gretchen's attorney made a motion to disallow any testimony from Martin, based upon the privilege of spousal immunity.

The Judge's interpretation of a principle of law would determine the outcome of the case.

The case went on for six straight hours. The Judge issued a bench decision. Gretchen was found guilty but the charges were reduced to a summary offense and she was fined the sum of $100 as punishment. Both Parnell and his lawyer opponent were exhausted at the end. As Parnell and Leslie walked out of the courtroom, Leslie looked at Parnell and asked, "Did we win?"

Challenge Questions:

1. How do you think the concept of "Spousal Immunity" applies to this case? Should Martin be prevented from testifying in this case?

2. Do you believe that Leslie's attorney's fee will be covered by her first party benefits in her homeowner's insurance policy? Further, do you believe that a claim against HDS's business liability policies can be made in this case?

3. Do you agree with the Judge's decision of imposing only a small fine and reducing the crime to a summary offense? Should Gretchen be punished more severely?

4. Legal issues aside, do you think Gretchen was within her moral rights to throw a punch at Leslie? (The Moral Issue).

Case Exercise 6D
Meatballs Gone Wild

After losing his job with a failed investment Bank, Ryan Rowland decided it was time for him to go out on his own. Together with a college friend, Kristin Tinges, (a securities broker who had worked with Ryan at BM Wagner) Rowland and Tinges organized a business named RT Securities, LLC. Ryan and Kristin bought furniture and equipment and rented a prime office space in the downtown area of a mid-sized community. They also hired two part time clerical employees and procured the service of a college intern named Rhett Volk. But how were they to get customers? After spending a few hours brainstorming they decided to throw a party and invite the rich and politically influential to attend. The partners rented a banquet room at the Bethallen Hotel and obtained the services of a local caterer, Striluck Caterers, a small business corporation owned and managed by Mavvie Striluck. Ryan and Kristin looked forward to the day of the party. They knew that such an event could make them or break them. But if all went well, the cost of the party (over $12,000) would be well worth it.

Two hundred guests were invited and expected to attend. According to industry standards, Striluck Caterers should have employed one server for each fifteen guests. But Mavvie thought thirteen servers would suffice. On the day of the party, disaster struck. An ice storm had swept through the area, knocking down trees and power lines, several homes and businesses lost power for the day, including the kitchens of Striluck Caterers. Mavvie knew that Ryan and Kristin were relying on her. But she needed the $11,000 catering fee. Without power, Mavvie did what she could using her gas grills and wood stove. The cheese puffs and cocktail weenies might not be up to par but she was determined to do her best to provide the food she promised for the party.

The storm created other problems as well. Of the thirteen servers expected to report to work that day, five called to say that they could not make it due to the storm and the icy road conditions. Two other servers just didn't come to work. Mavvie was in a panic. She asked one of her servers, Ashley Ciccone to recruit some of her college friends. Ashley was able to secure the services of Jordan Haverstock and Melissa Vinciguerra. Neither one had any server experience. However, both were eager to make money, especially since Melissa had lost her job as a carnie with the Harleysville traveling circus. Mavvie would have to go with eight servers instead of the recommended number but what else could she do?

At the party things went badly. The food clearly left something to be desired and the understaffed and inexperienced servers could not keep up with the requirements of their job. Guests were constantly complaining about the quality of the food and their inability to get drinks and service when needed. Things finally came to a head when Melissa tripped on a slippery part of the floor and dropped a hot, steaming plate of meatballs on Senator Gordon Stout and a guest to whom he was speaking, the influential journalist, Kyla Roderick. Both sustained second degree burns and had to be admitted to the emergency room at nearby St. Mamaluke's Hospital. In sum the party was a disaster.

Ryan and Kristin refuse to pay the $11,000 invoice for the catering services. Their claim is that the food was undercooked, poorly prepared – in particular the shrimp was underdone, the cheese puffs cool and the other food tasted bland and spoiled. Ryan and Kristin also contend that the service was atrocious due to the inexperience and gross negligence of the servers. They believe that Melissa was responsible to the injuries of their guests, Senator Stout and Kyla Roderick.

The contract between the parties provides for arbitration as the sole remedy in any breach of contract case. Here are the actors in the arbitration.

The Arbitrator (and his Assistant):

2 Attorneys for the claimants – Striluck Caterers

2 Attorneys for the respondents – RT Securities

Challenge Question:

Choose one of the roles above, prepare a case and role-play in the process. The Class will determine how each party performed in their parts. The persons with the best performance with receive 3 points each. The losers will receive 2 points as a consolation prize. ALL PARTIES HAVE SUBPOENA POWER.

CHAPTER 7
LEASES AND REAL ESTATE

Case Exercise 7A
Rental Property
A Good Investment?

Consider this: It is 15 years from now. You have been successful in your career and have a substantial sum of money to invest. Would you consider purchasing rental real estate? Let us assume that you are thinking about buying a beach house in a location, which would permit year around use. After reviewing the attached information, explain your opinion about becoming a dreaded "Landlord" in this situation.

You will find financial information at the end of this case.

Challenge Questions:

1. Using the financial information provided, do you think that owning this beach house is a good investment?

2. Given the generous tax breaks and preferences received by high wealth individuals to own rental real estate, do you think the system is fair and would you take advantage of it? (The Moral Issue).

Financial Information for Case Exercise 7A

Operating Income
Rentals
- LT Rentals (3 months x $1,500)	$ 4,500
- ST Rentals (20 weeks x $1,200)	$ 24,000
License Fees (70 days x $100)	$ 7,000

TOTAL INCOME   **$ 35,500**

Operating Expenses
Advertising	$ 300
Cleaning and Maintenance	$ 4,400
Commissions	$ 3,500
Insurance	$ 2,200
Legal and Prof Fees	$ 0
Management Fees	$ 0
Mortgage Interest	$ 0
Repairs	$ 2,000
Supplies	$ 4,000
Taxes	$ 3,600
Utilities	$ 2,690

Total Operating Expenses   **$ 22,690**

Depreciation Expenses
Property and Improvements	$ 5,145
Furniture and Fixtures	$ 13,714

Total Depreciation Expenses   **$ 18.859**

TOTAL EXPENSES   **$ 41,549**

TOTAL INCOME   **($ 6,049)**

Case 7B
A Christmas Eviction

Laura and Mark had found the perfect house in Lancaster. Mark's new job as a chemical engineer with American Compounds paid him twice as much as his old job at UEI Utilities. They could easily afford the new house without having to sell their old house first. Mark was making a lot of money now. Realizing that and believing that house values would increase, Laura and Mark decided to keep their old house in the west end of Allentown and rent it out. They thought the rental income would be another nice supplement to their income. As if they needed it!

Through an agent, they rented their old place to an unmarried couple. The lease was for 18 months starting March 1st and ending in August of the following year. The Lessees agreed to pay $1,000 per month. During the first four months, things were fine. The rent checks arrived on time and the couple seemed to be taking good care of the property. In July, however, they received a check for only $400 and one for $600 for the month of August. Checks in subsequent months increased, but were never for the full amount. They asked their attorney, James Parnell, to file a complaint in eviction. Parnell moved in quickly and by the end of September a *district justice judgment* had been entered against the Lessees. Parnell waited for the 30-day appeal period to end. He then filed for a *writ of possession*. The writ was issued and a *notice of eviction* was placed on the door of the house. At that point, one of the Lessees, Marcie Sweet, called Parnell and said, "Mr. Parnell, I was living here with my fiancé and he left me last June. I have been paying as much as I can afford each month, but my job at the insurance company doesn't pay a fortune and it is hard for me to balance my accounts each month. But please know this: anything I can afford I will pay each month. And whatever the balance is that I am deficient, I will pay to Laura and Mark eventually after I move out. But please Mr. Parnell, I need to stay here until next June at least. Then, I will move out."

Parnell passed this message on to his clients, but they were persistent that Marcie had to go. Indeed, they already met a man who had a good job at the regional electric company and he was willing to pay them $1,050 a month. On balance, Marcie was only giving them about 2/3 of what she owed each month. They wanted her out as soon as possible and wanted Parnell to get a judgment against her for the remaining balance. Parnell proceeded to get an *order of possession* from the district justice and contacted a constable working for the courts to assist him in removing Marcie and her possessions from the house, with physical force if necessary.

On December 23rd, two days before Christmas, Parnell and Constable Powers arrived at the house intending to execute the order. The house had a single strand of Christmas lights on the outside. Parnell could also see a small Christmas tree with modest decorations on it inside. Marcie begged him one last time to let her stay. Parnell stated that there was nothing he could do. "Give me just 30 minutes then I will leave". Parnell and the constable waited. Thirty minutes to the second, Marcie came out holding a little girl's hand. The pretty child looked like a tiny replica of her mother. The little girl was wearing a second hand coat and had earmuffs on to protect her from the cold. She was clutching her dolly and silent tears fell down her cheeks. At five years old, she already knew tragedy. Her daddy had left her mommy in the summer and now she had to leave her home, her neighborhood friends, and her school. Marcie exclaimed to Parnell as she packed her meager possessions in the back of her car, "Now do you understand me Mr. Parnell, I was only trying to let my daughter finish kindergarten. And I didn't want her to miss Christmas. She has been through enough." Parnell called his clients and explained the situation. Could they let her stay? "Definitely, no!" said Mark. "Get her and the kid out of there now. We have to make the house ready for our new tenant."

145

Marcie and her little girl drove away. They did not know their destination.

Challenge Questions:

1. Explain the process of eviction. What steps must you take to evict a tenant from your premises?

2. If you were Laura and Mark, would you have let Marcie stay until the end of the school year? (The Moral Issue).

Case 7C
The Endless Life Estate

Gwendolyn always wanted a house of her own. Finally, she had a decent job with benefits and had managed through hard effort to save a sum of money for a down payment. As a single woman, it wasn't easy. After months of looking, the realtor found a house that she thought would suit Gwen. The place had four acres; it was small but nicely kept. It had three bedrooms and two baths. The owner, Len Smart, had recently divorced and had received title in his own name as part of the property settlement agreement. It took a few days to do so, but Gwen managed to get Len down to a price that she could afford. But then Len broke the news to her.

The property was divided into two separately titled parcels. The parcels were right next to each other and were being sold together, but a run-down trailer was parked on parcel #2. Len told Gwen that his parents lived in the trailer and he didn't have the heart to ask them to leave. Besides they could not afford to go anywhere else. Len had promised them that they could live there until they passed away. But he had not anticipated the divorce. The trailer had been their home now for the last twenty years. Len's dad was 81 years old and his mother, Cora, was 77 at the time of the conveyance. Gwen asked her attorney, James Parnell, if he had any suggestions on how to handle this problem. She had met Len's parents and they seemed nice. Gwen certainly did not want to see them homeless.

Parnell suggested that Gwen receive title to parcel #1 on a fee simple absolute basis. An "Estate for Life" for parcel #2 was given to Len's parents; remainder would go to Gwen. Gwen thought that this solution was the best. After all, the parents were 81 and 77; how long could they live? Besides, Len moved to within ten miles of his parents and he promised to take care of them.

147

Within three years, Len's father died. But his mother continued to live and, at first, seemed fit and healthy. Gwen was increasingly worried about Cora and was constantly helping her with shopping, housework, and taking her to the doctor. Len lost his job, met another woman, married her and moved to California to take a new job. With Gwen next door, he felt better about leaving his mother behind. He promised to come home often, but he only returned once or twice a year. Gwen kept taking on more and more of the responsibility for Cora. As Cora's friends aged and passed away, things became even more difficult for Gwen. Gwen married as well. Her new husband, Frank, was also a nice and caring person. But Frank began to resent the predicament and especially resented the way Gwen had become the permanent caregiver to Cora. The trailer was not being well maintained and it was becoming a rusted out eye sore. Frank liked to keep a nice exterior to the house and it seemed like such a contrast to Cora's deteriorating abode.

Things came to a head. Frank had been stressed at work and decided that he wanted to go to the Virgin Islands for two weeks with his Christmas bonus. Naturally, he wanted Gwen to be with him. When presented the idea, at first Gwen seemed enthusiastic. However, upon reflection, Gwen said, "But Frank, Cora has at least five doctor's appointments in that time, and who will shop for her. She is 94 now and totally dependent on me. She will starve to death unless I make sure she eats." Frank responded, "Gwen, she isn't your mother, she is not a relative, and she is not your responsibility. You simply have a remainder interest in parcel #2. When she dies, the land is absolutely yours. Call Len and tell him to take care of his mother." Gwen did, but Len said it was not convenient for him to get to Pennsylvania in December. He would most likely be there in May. Gwen didn't know what to do. She wanted to go away with her husband and have a nice vacation. Frank threatened to go by himself if she didn't. Besides after 16 years of working

148

hard and taking care of Cora, she could use a break. But what if Cora died from exposure or illness or starvation while she was gone? There was a good chance she would.

Gwen did not know what to do.

Challenge Questions:

1. Explain how a life estate works. Also why is "remainder" called a future interest?

2. If you were Gwen and Frank, and wanted to finally get present title to the property, would you take a vacation knowing that there was a good chance that Cora would pass away? (The Moral Issue).

Case 7D
The Land on Morgan Court

Nick thought that Morgan Court was the perfect place to live. It was quiet and peaceful. The neighbors seemed to mind their own business. With his wife of fourteen years, his four children, and their pets, he moved into the recently constructed house.

Nick and his family set out to improve the property. After a few months, the lawn was manicured, the bushes sculpted, and the grass was nearly perfect. Next to the house was an open field with a few trees on it. Some of the trees were alive and some were dead. Nick had only met his neighbor once. She was a woman in her 50s. Her adult children would come by every now and then to bring her groceries and other essential items. The children clearly were making an effort to keep up with the maintenance of the yard as well, but they often would not show up for weeks at a time.

The climax came one summer day in July. Nick's daughter, Patty, was celebrating her ninth birthday. Nick had invited his large extended family as well as a number of Patty's friends to a party. His neighbor's property was a mess, so Nick and his teenage son Mike, took the initiative to mow the neighbor's lawn, and trim the bushes and trees. While in the process of doing so, the neighbor's daughter happened to come by and told Nick he was welcome to maintain the property at any time. The field covered almost 3/4 of an acre, but Nick had the equipment and stamina to complete the job. After a while, Nick became the sole party responsible for the maintenance of the property. As the property improved under Nick's care, he began having more outdoor parties, using the field for picnic tables and outdoor games. For all intents and purposes the field had become Nick's possession.

Two years following the time at which he moved in, Nick's neighbor was committed to a mental institution because of her illness. It was believed that she intended to come back, but she never did. Nick, in an effort to coordinate his landscaping, placed a border of bushes between the neighbor's house and the property belonging to his neighbor, which he was maintaining. After 25 years, Nick was thinking seriously of getting a new survey done of his property, using the bush line as his far property line. The additional land would double the size of his lot and increase the values of his property by at least 25%. Morgan Court was proving to be both a great place to live and a good investment for Nick.

Challenge Questions:

1. What possible legal theory could be used by Nick to permit him to claim a part of his neighbor's property?

2. Assuming Nick can make good faith claim to the property, it ethical to take your neighbor's land, even if you had made maintained the property for all those years? (The Moral Issue).

Case 7E
An Afternoon with Adelaide

Megabusiness, Incorporated, a fortune 500 Company, decided that the upper bucks county region of Pennsylvania was where they wanted to locate their facility. Megabusiness purchased a large agricultural tract near the major highways leading to both the Philadelphia and Lehigh Valley areas. Megabusiness intended to use the facility for light manufacturing, assembly, and distribution and back office support for their Connecticut corporate headquarters. The Controller for Megabusiness estimated that the land costs were only 1/10 of what they would be in New England for similarly situated property. Megabusiness only intended to use 1/3 of the property for its own use; the other 2/3 would be sold in small pieces to other commercial and industrial enterprises after its facility was finished. In essence Megabusiness was acting as a commercial property developer as well and its potential returns from the activities were expected to easily pay for the total costs of the project, including all the cost for its land, construction and necessary services. It was a good business decision.

The problem: the land was land-locked. Eleven property owners controlled the road frontage and parcels leading into the area. For Megabusiness to complete its project, the company needed to purchase all parcels prior to its submission of a development plan for final government approval, which was expected without controversy. James Parnell, an attorney with a medium sized Pennsylvania law firm was asked to work alongside a real estate agent acting as an agent for an undisclosed principal. Ten of the parcels were purchased from the homeowners and landowners for approximately twice the fair market appraised value of the properties. Total costs for the project were estimated to be $25,000,000 of which $2,000,000 was budgeted for additional land costs (4% of the total project). The 11th piece of property presented a problem for Parnell. A farmer (more than willing to sell) currently owned it, however in doing a title search Parnell discovered that the land was sold by sheriff's sale in 1947 and that the sheriff had failed to post the legally required notice of the sale. Hence there was a title problem with the land.

Parnell had two choices, he could bring an action to quiet title, but such an action might take up to a year to complete, assuming no one filed an objection or responsive pleading. Time was money and Megabusiness stood to lose big with such a delay. The other option Parnell possessed was to track down the descendants of the bankrupt farmer and purchase their potential interests in the property through a "Quit Claim Deed". After a thorough investigation, it was discovered that the only remaining living descendant of the farmer was his daughter, Adelaide Malveux. Megabusiness was willing to pay a sum of up to $100,000 to purchase Adie's interest and complete its land acquisition needs as quickly as possible.

Adelaide was 83 years old. She had been married for many years, but her husband had died when Adelaide was in her 50s and she had never remarried. They had one child from the marriage, a son, but he had died in the Vietnam War. Thus, she had no children or grandchildren. An only child herself, she did not have siblings, nieces or nephews.

Adelaide had spent most of her life working as a church choir director. She was also an accomplished organist. While this occupation brought much satisfaction to her life, it brought very little in the way of economic value. At 83 Adie was living on a very small pension from her church and a meager monthly social security check. She was living in an assisted living facility in Eastern Berks County. She was, at the point, considered a charity case since her monthly income could no longer pay her monthly expenses at the home. Regardless, the church-affiliated home maintained a commitment to her care until her passing.

Parnell had done his homework well. He spoke with pastors and others with whom Adie had worked. They all described her as a compassionate and delightful person. Parnell prepared a "Quit Claim Deed "and called the home to arrange an appointment with Adie. In his initial telephone conversation with Adie, she did not seem to understand the reason for Parnell's call or his interest for her late father's farm, which had long ago been sold. Parnell advised Adie to seek the advice of her own legal counsel prior to his visit. Adie did not do so. Parnell and Adie agreed to meet in person on Friday afternoon at her place of residence in Berks County.

When Parnell arrived at the home, he was relieved to meet a friendly and hospitable woman. Adie was old, small and frail but she still had a pleasant smile and alert eyes. Adie had even made tea and baked muffins in the home's kitchen area for Parnell. Parnell spent the next two hours talking to Adie and asking questions about her life and her work with religious music. With no living relatives to speak of and few surviving friends, it was clear that the time spent together was a welcomed break for Adie. Parnell also enjoyed his "Tea Party" with Adie. He promised to visit her again. But the time came for business. Parnell painstakingly explained the issue to Adie and the reason for his visit there. After 30 minutes or so, Adie was finally getting it. Once again, Parnell advised Adie about her right to counsel. Adie explained that she neither desired a lawyer nor did she have the means to pay for one. Besides, Adie told Parnell that he seemed like such a nice young man and that she certainly trusted him. Parnell, assessing the situation, offered Adie $500 if she would sign the "Quit Claim Deed" to Megabusiness. Adie agreed and thanked Parnell for the money. She could certainly use it.

The project was completed on time and ahead of budget. It proved to be a great investment for Megabusiness, Incorporated. Parnell had done his job.

Challenge Questions:

1. Explain the use of quitclaim deeds in this case. Further, how do "Actions to Quiet Title" help real estate developers move their projects along?

2. Based upon your understanding of the Rules of Professional Conduct, which govern the activities of Attorneys, did Parnell fulfill his ethical and professional duty to this client, Megabusiness, Incorporated?

3. In your opinion, was there a disconnect between attorney ethics and the ethics of most human beings in this case? Further, do you believe the client should authorize the attorney to make a more generous settlement if asked to do so? (The Moral Issue).

CHAPTER 8
SECURED TRANSACTIONS

Case 8A
Repossession On A Fine Summer Day

Darren Quigley wasn't even sure how much debt he had any more. Darren was a licensed surveyor and business appeared good. Certainly, he was busy. But between lawsuits and payroll costs, it just didn't seem like he could ever get ahead financially. Darren thought of himself as a good surveyor but he never did like the business end of it.

Finally, after obtaining a large receivable from a developer-client, Darren had a positive cash balance in his company's bank account - a surplus of $16,000. Sure, he should have paid his bills first, but Darren decided as hard as he was working he deserved a nice vacation. He cleaned out the business account and used the money to take his wife, children and parents-in-law to Bermuda for the week (and a good time was had by all). When he returned the usual correspondence and demands from creditors was waiting for him. They would have to be patient if they wanted to be paid.

The President of the First National Bank of Reilly City finally had enough. He had given Darren fair warning on multiple occasions and had tried to reschedule his debts. But Darren was no longer paying on the $50,000 working capital note that he had issued to the bank. The time had come for action. The bank's law firm was called and James Parnell, an experienced bank attorney, was given the job of collecting on Darren's debt. Fortunately, the bank had secured the note with an airtight security agreement with Darren and had filed a UCC 1 against all of his business equipment as part of the loan package.

Parnell knew that the surveying equipment was very valuable. Indeed the "Topcon 4 Survey Instrument" itself was worth at least $30,000, even though it was now five years old. Parnell provided copies of the security agreement and public filing to Ken Manley, along with a letter of authority from his law firm acting for the bank. The letter requested that Manley seize the surveying equipment. Manley, an ex-marine, was employed as a police sergeant for a local municipality and handled repossession work as a side business after his shift was completed.

Darren knew that creditors might attempt to repossess his equipment. He made sure that the equipment was never out of his reach or that of a trusted assistant. When the day was done, the surveying equipment was promptly locked up in the trunk of his 4 by 4. Manley had been attempting to seize the equipment for weeks, but could not get it. Darren was always one step ahead of him.

Manley demanded a meeting with Parnell. He was trying his best, but he didn't see a way to peaceably obtain the equipment and he knew that Darren would never give his consent to the repossession. What could he do? Parnell had an idea. Jennifer Albright, a 19-year-old student at Berks College, was working as an intern that summer for Parnell's law firm. What if picnic tables and a bench were placed in the row of trees on the farmland next to the site where Darren and his crew were working on that August day? Parnell asked Jennifer is she was willing to be part of the plan. Jennifer was happy to help. A table was set up in the shade. Lemonade, iced tea and cookies were placed on the table. As expected, the crew could not resist flirting with Jennifer. As the men approached her Jennifer explained that she was planning on having a picnic and was just waiting for her girlfriends. She acted in a friendly manner and invited the men to sit down and take a break from their work activities. Soon, Darren and all of his workers were sitting happily with Jennifer and enjoying the shade and drinks.

Manley, observing the day's actions from a distant perch, saw his chance. He slowly drove his vehicle up to the site and before they realized it, seized the equipment. Darren was furious.

Challenge Questions:

1. Are Manley's actions in the seizure of the equipment lawful under Article 9 of the Uniform Commercial Code?

2. Do you think that Parnell's trick on Darren was ethically proper? (The Moral Issue).

Case 8B
The Sad Case of Tim Glynn

When Tim Glynn left college, the world seemed like a wonderful place. Due to a great class he had called "Finance and Credit" Tim found a good job as a commercial lender at MegaBank International. Within ten years of graduation, he was making a nice six-figure income with good benefits. He also found and fell in love with the woman of his dreams, Stephanie Paulson. Marriage to Steph followed and he saw a bright future with the wonderful Steph. They had also bought a nice and house and Steph told him expect a family in the future, the doctor was sure of it. All looked great from his perch on the 18th floor of Megabank. It seemed like life could hardly get better. Little did Tim know?

Among his best clients was the Skorton Brothers Corporation (SBC) a large regional business specializing in the import and distribution of prosthetic devices. Tim had helped the Skortons reach the top with creative financing that helped the start-up company secure the capital it needed to further its rapid expansion. The Skorton Brothers, wishing to show their appreciation to Tim, talked him into going on an "all expenses paid trip" to Las Vegas with them and one of their mutual friends from college, Andrew Messcreation. Tim wasn't sure he wanted to go without Steph but the Skortons wouldn't take no for an answer. No wives or girlfriends would be allowed to accompany the crew.

In Vegas, the boys had a good time until one night when things got out of hand. Andrew insisted that Tim drink to excess and attend a private party that he and the Skortons were throwing in their hotel suite. Tim, unaccustomed to alcohol, consumed too much – to the point where his judgment was impaired. In addition, there were several women attendees at the party who were supposedly friends of Andrew but were of suspicious and nefarious backgrounds. When Tim awoke in the suite the next morning he realized that there was a woman next to him and that he had violated the sacred oath he had made to Steph at their wedding ceremony. Tim decided to say nothing to Steph and felt sure that neither Andrew nor the Skortons would say anything. After all, what happens in Vegas stays in Vegas. Tim was wrong.

The Vice-President of SBC, Casey Schwepps, had been told of Tim's exploits by one of the Skortons in confidence. However, Casey had coincidentally known Steph from their college days and was outraged by Tim's conduct. She told Steph who promptly filed for divorce, alimony, and child support for little Tim as well as a claim for all of their marital property and legal fees. Steph, represented by James Parnell, was successful in her claims. To make matters worse, the VP of Megabank, Greg Scarlet, discovered Tim's actions in Vegas (again the source was Casey). Greg summarily fired Tim for violating the bank's strict "Code of Conduct" with customers.

With no job, no property, support payment etc. Tim is now in real bad financial condition. He has run up close to $80,000 in credit card debts and another $20,000 in unsecured lines of credit at the bank. He has recently found another position as a lender at a regional bank but at a junior level and at less than half of what he was making at Megabank.

Challenge Questions:

1. Assume that Tim's unsecured debt is held by one lender
    and that the account is close to $110,000 with interest and
    fees: you are the work out specialist assigned to handle
    Tim's file – what actions would you take?

2. Given Tim's personal situation, would you be willing to
    close the file and forego any effort at collections? Further,
    if you were Stephanie Paulson, would you be willing to
    take Tim back if he asked for forgiveness? (The Moral
    Issue).

Case 8C
The Land Contract

Julie and Brian were parents again. Julie knew that their cramped apartment would not do. They were already much too crowded. Where would they even put the new baby? The problem was money, as usual. But Julie was sick and tired of delayed gratification; she wanted a house, one way or the other.

Between taking care of the children and helping out her blind husband, Julie was not able to work herself. Brian was an assistant professor at Carlisle College in Minnesota. Brian loved what he did and Julie was proud that he has able to complete a Ph.D. and obtain a full time teaching position in psychology. But Brian's salary was all they had to live on and it wasn't much.

One day Julie was reading the real estate section, as usual. She saw an advertisement "BY OWNER, House on 1/2 acre near Carlisle College, Owner willing to finance or accept Sale on Contract arrangement". Julie drove by the address of the property on her way to the shopping center. The location of the house was perfect. It was just two blocks from the college, an easy walk for Brian. The house was modest and needed a lot of work but she called the owner anyway. The owner, Leon Bass, liked Julie. After a few days of negotiation, they agreed on a sales price of $100,000.00. Since Julie had next to nothing for a down payment, Leon agreed to permit a "Sale on Contract" basis for the financing. He agreed to accept 120 monthly payments of $1213 a month (an imputed discount rate of 8%). Julie and Brian signed the contract and moved into their new home.

After 5 and 1/2 years of living in the property, Julie and Brian had done a lot to improve it. They installed a white picket fence and totally redecorated the inside with paint, wallpaper and new carpeting throughout. Julie also landscaped the property (the children loved to help). Brian seemed to be on his way to getting tenure. While they struggled sometimes financially, overall Julie was happy with her life. Then it happened. Brian was teaching a senior seminar when he lost consciousness and collapsed in class. One of his students called 911. Brian was taken to the hospital. He had a massive heart attack. The doctors made it clear that while Brian might recover, he would need years of rest and medical care and could not work during that time. Carlisle College put Brian into their long-term disability program. Brian was now only making 50% of his modest salary. Julie could no longer afford the monthly payments on the house.

Leon did not know what to do. He came to rely on that money. In order to consider his options, Leon had a realtor appraise the house. Between inflation and the improvements Julie made, the house was now worth $180,000. It was Leon's right to ask Julie and Brian to leave the house, since they had defaulted on the contract. Leon had to make a decision.

Challenge Questions:

1. Explain how the "Land Contract" or "Sale on Contract" differs from a mortgage or "Deed of Trust" as a form of security interest.

2. If you were Leon, would you repossess the property and force Julie and Brian (and their children) out of the house? (The Moral Issue).

Case Exercise 8D
Metzger Bottling Company

Assume the Following:

Metzger Bottling Company is a privately held company. While sales of its non-alcoholic drinks have been strong in recent years, its financial situation has deteriorated. A regional company with sales of $350,000,000; its expenses have exceeded its revenue for every year in the past eight. Approximately $160,000,000 of its expenses is in the form of employee costs. Of its 950 employees, approximately 650 are in either a blue-collar union or staff support union. The union has negotiated a very generous "defined benefit" pension and a traditional "fee for service" health plan for its members. The company has historically provided the non-union employees with the same type of benefits. Employees can presently retire at full benefits at age 55 and remain in the company health plan until they are Medicare eligible at 65. Pension, health and legacy costs now account for $75,000,000 a year.

The company has frozen employment levels and squeezed vendors to reduce its other costs. Despite these efforts, in 2014 the company lost $20,000,000. 2015 shapes up to be worse. The income statement and balance sheet are attached to this case.

The company will run out of cash by the end of this quarter. It cannot issue equity and needs to deal with its creditors as soon as possible. A law firm has recently been contacted to discuss the issue of bankruptcy with the board. The company would prefer not to take this route and does not want the idea of bankruptcy to circulate outside the boardroom at this time. However, it has not dismissed the option.

Challenge Questions:

1. Your group specializes in financial "work-outs". The bank approaches you as its consultant about the problems of the company. Under its covenants with the bank, the company is obliged to follow the bank's recommendations. What strategy would you use to resolve the company's financial problems? Pay particular attention to the issue of employee benefits and the labor relations tensions that may result in a restructuring.

2. You are the bargaining agent for the union. The company approaches you through its bank appointed consultant to enter into re-negotiations. What strategy would you employ to protect your members?

3. If you were Nicolette Metzger, the 21 year-old granddaughter and heiress to the stock of the company, would you attempt to adjust your financial structure and save the company and its workers; or would you sell the company for its approximate equity value of $15,000,000 and get out of town? (The Moral Issue).

Balance Sheet
Metzger Bottling Company
12/31/15

	2015	2014
Cash & Deposit	$6,000,000.00	$13,000,000.00
Marketable Securities	$2,000,000.00	$5,000,000.00
Inventory	$15,500,000.00	$16,000,000.00
Raw Materials	$6,500,000.00	$6,200,000.00
Property & Equipment	$162,000,000.00	$171,000,000.00
Intangibles	$1,500,000.00	$1,700,000.00
Total Assests	**$193,500,000.00**	**$212,900,000.00**
Accounts Payable	$11,000,000.00	$10,500,000.00
Accrued Expenses	$14,500,000.00	$14,200,000.00
Income Taxes	$900,000.00	$200,000.00
Notes Payable	$28,000,000.00	$30,600,000.00
Long Term Debt	$83,000,000.00	$84,000,000.00
Deferred Charges	$41,100,000.00	$38,000,000.00
Total Liabilities	**$178,500,000.00**	**$177,500,000.00**
Total Equity	**$15,000,000.00**	**$35,400,000.00**

Income Statement
Metzer Bottling Company
12/31/15

	2015	2014
Gross Sales	$350,000,000.00	$356,000,000.00
Cost of Goods Sold	-$115,000,000.00	-$111,000,000.00
R&D Expenditures	-$1,500,000.00	-$3,000,000.00
Employment Expenses	-$160,000,000.00	-$165,000,000.00
Employment Legacy Costs	-$75,000,000.00	-$61,000,000.00
Depreciation and Amortization	-$9,000,000.00	-$500,000.00
Interest Expenses	-$9,500,000.00	-$9,100,000.00
Income Taxes	$0.00	-$1,300,000.00
Total Income	**-$20,000,000.00**	**$5,100,000.00**

Made in the USA
Middletown, DE
15 January 2021